Foreword

The White Paper, *Better Schools*, published in March 1985, called for action to improve standards of education in our schools. Systematic evaluation and appraisal of the performance of schools and teachers, coupled with a more extensive and more effective in-service training network, has an important part to play in improving standards. The Department organised a conference in November 1985 to concentrate attention on the need for evaluation and appraisal in the interests of raising standards, and to promote the active participation in the work that is needed at all levels — schools, local education authorities and central government.

The conference papers in this volume are published for the same purpose. They were written by people who know and understand the school system. I am most grateful to them. I commend the papers to all those seeking to improve the quality of school education.

Sir Keith Joseph
Secretary of State for Education
and Science

CONTENTS

PRESENTATION 5

Introduction

The purpose of this publication is to make available to a wider audience the papers prepared for a two-day residential conference convened by the Department of Education and Science and held in Birmingham in November 1985. The conference was a follow-up to the White Paper *Better Schools*[1].

Better Schools called for action:

— to secure greater clarity about the objectives and content of the curriculum;

— to reform the examination system and improve assessment so that they promote more effectively the objectives of the curriculum, the achievements of pupils, and the recording of those achievements;

— to improve the professional effectiveness of teachers and the management of the teaching force;

— to reform school government and to harness more fully the contribution which can be made to good school education by parents, employers and others outside the education service.

Schools, local education authorities (LEAs) and central government all have contributions to make towards achieving these goals and assessing progress towards them. The purpose of the conference was to consider the responsibilities of these three agencies for monitoring, evaluating and appraising the achievements of schools and teachers.

The conference was built round five presentations to plenary sessions. Each presentation was followed by discussion, and issues arising were also discussed by participants in small groups. The papers prepared for the plenary sessions are reprinted in this volume. A brief note of some points arising is offered below.

PLENARY SESSIONS

1. The School's Task and the Teacher's Task

In the opening presentation, *Professor Taylor* argued that the ultimate test of any policy or initiative was whether it secured real improvement in the individual school and classroom. That did not mean that a systematic framework was not an essential means to that end. Professor Taylor said that in his view, even among those who for various reasons objected to systematic evaluation and appraisal, there

---

[1] Cmnd 9469, HMSO, March 1985.

were a large number of widely shared assumptions about what pupils of a given age should be taught and should learn. It was the responsibility of the Secretary of State and of the local authorities to provide the framework within which better schools could be created and progress could be monitored; but it was the task of the profession to bring about improvement where it really counted — in the school and the individual classroom.

The discussion that followed revealed widespread support for this view. Teachers needed to be able to do their work confident that their aims and objectives were widely shared, and confident that they themselves possessed the necessary skills supported by appropriate in-service training and research.

2. Assessment Techniques and Approaches

SCI Mr Bolton's presentation offered an overview of seven technical papers which discussed various approaches to assessing the performance of pupils, teachers and schools — public examinations, records of achievement, testing, the work of the Assessment of Performance Unit (APU), inspection, teacher appraisal, and whole school evaluation. He argued that there was little disagreement with the general idea that the work of the education system should be subject to a range of assessments. The important questions concerned the ways in which those assessments should be made. There was much useful work in hand to develop further the many existing useful techniques and instruments for assessment.

Mr Bolton identified a number of key issues. There was a need to take further current work on the development of agreed curricular objectives, particularly for the primary phase, as a cornerstone of constructive and effective assessment; assessment techniques which might harmfully influence teaching and learning should be avoided; a more systematic pattern for LEA procedures for inspection and reporting seemed desirable; work on school self-evaluation and teacher appraisal was patchy and still at a stage where much more work on the development of effective and acceptable instruments and techniques was required.

In the course of discussion Mr Bolton agreed with participants that curricular flexibility was desirable; that there had been an enormous increase in the achievements of many primary school pupils over the last 30 years; that social and economic background factors had a strong influence on achievement level of different pupils. But some current curricular inflexibilities in secondary schools — for example, boys still missing out on foreign languages and girls missing out on science — could not be justified. In primary schools, too, there was a large gap between the curricular provision and achievements of the best and that of the rest. Such considerations reinforced the case for developing agreed curricular objectives, monitoring progress, and assessing achievements. Environmental factors had to be taken into account when assessing school and pupil achievements, and although a good deal of work had been done on this further work was needed.

3. The Role and Responsibility of the School

For the third plenary session *Miss Marshall* presented a brief overview of four papers by headteachers (who contributed to the ensuing discussion). These papers provided pictures of schools engaged in various forms of curriculum review, pupil assessment and teacher appraisal, and made it clear that in practice all these aspects of school evaluation were closely connected. The real-life experiences of assessment presented in them offered many messages, and Miss Marshall stressed the need for a school to be at an appropriate stage of professional readiness to embark successfully on any substantial programme of staff appraisal and self-evaluation. Miss Marshall offered a checklist of what seemed to be required to promote a national framework for constructive school evaluation and a system of appraising teachers that would be both effective and fair:

— an efficient and flexible staff training programme;

— the availability of critical professional advice from outside the schools themselves;

— guidelines on curricular aims and criteria for assessment and appraisal negotiated and agreed locally;

— adequate material resources and appropriate working conditions;

— recognition of the demands on time, particularly of teachers and of LEA services, realistically costed in a programme of development for an area;

— acceptance by the schools that capacity to benefit from support implied an openness to outside views, particularly those of parents and the local community.

In the discussion following the presentation there was widespread support for the view that adequate preparation was essential, so that schools could be both willing and ready before embarking on assessment programmes. The emphasis should be on the positive aspects of teacher appraisal, and on the provision of associated in-service training; only then could appraisal be attractive to the teachers. A key central government responsibility was the provision of adequate resources matching the required rate of progress.

4. The Role and Responsibility of the LEA

For the fourth presentation *Mr Graham* and *Mr Johnson* offered papers concentrating on teacher appraisal and on whole school evaluation respectively. Mr Graham argued that the best form of assessment was self-assessment, and that any institutional framework should be in support of this. He considered that systematic teacher appraisal could reap considerable benefits, provided that certain ingredients were in place: a set of national criteria to ensure consistency of application and in time some national validity for findings; LEA support; and an appraisal scheme negotiated openly on a basis of partnership and trust. A successful scheme would require close co-operation between schools, LEAs and central government. The resource cost of a credible teacher appraisal scheme would be significant, and it was essential that this should be met, and be seen to be met.

Mr Johnson was confident that school self-assessment could be developed on the basis of criteria with national validity. But local schemes should be based on co-operative action among those directly affected. Particular importance attached to the role of the headteacher and advice from a strong local authority advisory service.

Discussion centred on the extent to which national criteria and LEA guidelines might hinder enterprise and initiative at the school level. There were various opinions on this issue, but the general view was that a sensible system would need some form of national framework. The idea of separate and perhaps different school evaluation and teacher appraisal schemes for each of the LEAs in England and Wales was not attractive.

5. The Role and Responsibility of the Secretary of State

In the final plenary session *Sir Keith Joseph* began by saying that, although he would be speaking largely about measures that could be undertaken only from the centre, such measures were valuable only if they helped to improve what went on in the classroom. It was the Government's task to promote the achievement of agreement about curricular objectives, and seek to set out the extent of the agreement reached as guidance for LEAs, schools, teachers, teacher trainers and examination boards. Government policy statements, such as that on science published early in 1985, and the HMI 'Curriculum Matters' series of which five had so far been published, were intended to support that purpose. Dealing directly with evaluation and appraisal of schools and pupils' achievements, Sir Keith noted that Government provided two distinct services: HMI inspection and the work of the APU. On the development of a teacher appraisal scheme, he emphasised that what he had in mind was a carefully worked out and introduced scheme, embodying safeguards for individual teachers, linked to the provision of in-service training and the career development of teachers.

In the course of the ensuing discussion Sir Keith Joseph argued that the proposed legislation for the appraisal of teachers should not be seen as threatening, and stressed its enabling nature. He shared the view that school and teacher appraisal systems should be introduced voluntarily. He argued, however, that it was desirable to have a national framework in which local appraisal schemes would operate. Turning to the issue of resources, he agreed that additional resources would be needed, among other things for in-service training and teacher time spent on appraisal work. Pilot schemes would help to quantify these needs, and he hoped that progress could be made before long in developing such pilot schemes.

DISCUSSION GROUPS

The following paragraphs provide a brief summary of the main points which arose in the various discussion groups.

Two themes ran through all the discussions. The first related to the conference itself. Although, with few exceptions, participants supported the view that school and teacher assessment systems had a contribution to make to improving what was offered to pupils, the conference was not in a position to endorse any specific proposals.

The second was that the provision of adequate resources was essential if worthwhile systems of assessing the work of teachers and schools were to be established.

The groups considered four main topics: whole school evaluation; teacher appraisal; the allocation of responsibility in this area between schools and LEAs; and the responsibilities of government. These topics are dealt with below.

Whole School Evaluation

This was seen as a fast-developing activity. Most participants were in favour of it, provided that the purposes of the evaluation were clearly seen by the teachers as supportive and not threatening. Evaluation had to be against a list of agreed objectives. There were differing views about whether these objectives should spring from work in individual schools or be laid down by some combination of the LEA and the Government, but the general view seemed to be that many of the objectives had to come from within the school itself, but also fall within a broad national framework. The difficult task was to create such a framework, offering appropriate guidance without hindering enterprising developments at the school level.

It was generally agreed that the need for assessment must not be allowed to determine objectives. It was clear that much of what was important in the learning process could not be measured objectively. But such factors as emotional and aesthetic development should not be discounted because of measurement difficulties. While much of any school assessment process would necessarily be based on the achievements of pupils, care must be taken to avoid putting too much weight on what was readily measurable. It was considered that developments with records of achievement were beginning to make helpful progress with the monitoring of performance in some of the less readily measurable areas of learning.

The particular problems of evaluation at the primary phase were discussed at length. The difficulty of establishing what breadth of curriculum should be offered meant that the framework for evaluation could not easily be set. There might be a tendency to give too much emphasis to assessing the quality of teaching. This would be further encouraged by the knowledge that much achievement by primary pupils was not readily measurable, and the allied fact that there were very few trained in the skills of primary school assessment. The recent trend towards setting out more clearly and formally school aims might help provide a better basis for the more general evaluation of performance.

As to who should be involved in the evaluation process, the general view was that all the professional staff in school, including in particular the headteacher, should take part. Beyond that, the role of governors, parents, outside experts and the local authority itself had to be established. There were some reservations about involving governors and parents in the actual appraisal process.

Teacher Appraisal

There was general agreement that the ultimate aim of teacher appraisal must be to improve learning by pupils. But there was debate about the extent to which the appraisal of teachers could or should be detached from the promotion process. There was complete support for the view that any appraisal scheme should aid the professional development of teachers, and some participants believed that an appraisal system could be devised which would achieve this and also help identify and prepare teachers for promotion. Others believed that the linking of these two functions would result in a scheme seen as threatening by many teachers.

There was general agreement that performance across all the main aspects of a teacher's work should be assessed. For this to be done the observation of classroom performance was seen as a necessary part of the appraisal process. Pupil achievement provided one important criterion in appraising teacher performance, but there was concern that the search for measurable criteria might lead to a narrow conception of what made a good teacher.

A large measure of confidence between the schools, LEAs and the Government itself was seen as essential to the development of a successful teacher appraisal scheme. While many argued that a successful scheme had to have the support of professional staff and therefore to some extent had to be developed in the school itself, it was generally accepted that this was not inconsistent with the setting of a national framework and the development of national criteria in order to avoid a proliferation of separately designed schemes (which could cause problems of acceptability across local authority boundaries). It was emphasised that these criteria should be broad, flexible and based on experience from a number of pilot schemes. It was considered that a fully developed national scheme would take two to three years to design.

Responsibilities of the School and the LEA

Many participants considered that the initiative for assessment schemes, whether of the whole school or just the teacher, best came from individual schools. Local authority intervention was seen as being necessary only if the voluntary development of assessment schemes slowed down, or for particular activities such as the appraisal of a headteacher. Having said this, participants were also clear that the development of a scheme should be collaborative, using assistance available from local authorities and working within agreed national guidelines.

The evidence a school would require to satisfy itself that its assessment schemes were proceeding along sensible lines should be expected to include observation of changes in classroom practice. This evidence would however often be subjective, and there was benefit to be gained from establishing goals for specific areas of the curriculum. Schools would need to have a continuing interchange of ideas with other schools, and support from local authority advisers.

The views of the 'customers' were regarded as being important: above all the pupils themselves, but also parents, governors and local employers. In considering the presentation of school evaluation reports, it was clear that full reports should be made to the staff, the governors and the LEA. There was no clear view about the evidence an LEA needs to satisfy itself that its schools and teachers are performing adequately, although the need for monitoring information was recognised. Participants were clear, however, that LEAs had particular responsibilities for disseminating good practice among their schools, and providing appropriate expertise and resources.

The Responsibility of Government

The role of government was seen to be that of creating the appropriate climate and framework, and there was concern that the Government might be seeking change too quickly, and without sufficient resources. The development of a teacher appraisal scheme was being promoted in difficult times and it was important that it be introduced voluntarily.

It was recognised that the Government required evidence that the performance of the education system was satisfactory. The main provider of this evidence was seen as HM Inspectorate. HMI reports were generally helpful. It was also thought appropriate for government to seek views from the various client groups — parents, employers, and the pupils themselves.

Conclusion

The conference showed widespread support for the further development of assessment systems as a means of improving what is offered to school pupils. The challenge to the system — schools, LEAs and central government — is to find the best means to that end.

The School's Task and the Teacher's Task

Professor William Taylor, CBE, Vice-Chancellor, University of Hull

Contexts for change

Better Schools reflects a movement of thought and action that began in the post-oil shock and inflation-bedevilled mid-seventies. Two decades of post-war growth had fuelled an explosion of economic and social expectations, especially on the part of a generation with no direct experience of the Depression of the thirties or the deprivations of war. To satisfy these expectations depended increasingly on the successful application of science and technology to production and the provision of services, generating labour requirements and employment pressures with which existing structures of education and training were ill-equipped to deal.

Greater social and geographical mobility underlined disparities in educational opportunity between one part of the country and another. A more participative approach to school government stimulated interest in educational outcomes. New research exposed the limitations of earlier work which had spawned the oversimplified notion that 'teachers don't make a difference'. Variations in performance were revealed between apparently similar schools a few miles apart.

Other contributory factors included demographic downturn; the rise of consumerism, with its stress on value for money; anxieties about international competition, especially from Japan; awkward questions about how far our educational provision was responsible for past economic decline and would be a brake on future competitive capacity, and realisation that the impact of investment in curriculum reform had been diminished by lack of attention to the initial and in-service training of those who would implement classroom change.

All this, coupled with the problems of living in a complex, crowded, multicultural and largely urban environment, highlighted apparent weaknesses in the educational accomplishments of school leavers and adults alike. To those who asserted that our schools were good, the question was increasingly put, 'Are they good enough?' For all those who realised that neither utopia nor nostalgia would suffice, there was urgent need to see what could be done about the imperfect present.

Policies for improvement

The ultimate test of any policy or initiative is whether it secures real improvement where it really counts — in the school, the classroom and the learning of the individual pupil. Improvement starts and ends with the pupil.

Quality of teaching is a vital element in such learning. Quality of management, administration and leadership, in department and in school, in local authority and nationally, also play their part. But a successful policy for school improvement is to be judged not just on legislative and regulative measures, or the beefing up of national and local inspectorates, the reform of examinations, the more active involvement of parents and governors. The test of all these measures is whether they improve what goes on between nine to four and beyond, for forty or more weeks a year, in tens of thousands of individual classrooms, laboratories, workshops, gymnasia and other places where teachers and students gather together for the purpose of learning and teaching — and what difference it all makes to the lives of those so educated. It is this that needs to be evaluated and appraised.

Any programme for school improvement has to have a feel for the day-to-day realities of education, of what it is like to enter a new and strange environment at age five; to encounter that mixture of success and failure, frustration and elation, ennui and joy that accompany any effort at any age to turn information into knowledge and understanding and to acquire new skills; to relate the culture and values of street and tower block to those of secondary school, the fantasies of novel and video to city and suburban living; to confront the prospects of career or of unemployment; to come to terms with one's own sexuality and racial and social identity; to cope with the complexities of what has happened to the family in the late 20th century.

Policy has to be sensitive to how such realities affect the teaching and learning of the unique individual. It has to reckon with what it is like for a teacher to face 4C on a wet Friday afternoon after a cancelled games period, to share with students the satisfaction that comes from a challenge mastered, to feel the exhaustion that active involvement in learning entails, to experience the anxieties, the hopes and the despair inseparable from full engagement in any task involving other people's futures.

It is harder in a democracy to secure agreement to policies that emanate from governments than to those which have their origins in reports of advisory councils or professional bodies. A politicised world and a free press live by conflict rather than consensus. It is inevitable, therefore, that the intentions to secure improvement set out in *Better Schools* have come in for criticism. If what is proposed is to engage as many as possible of those concerned with the task of the school and the task of the teacher, these criticisms need to be identified and addressed.

The critics' views

Five criticisms of current policies are worthy of comment.

The *first* has to do with the rightness and wisdom of intervention from the centre in what is taught in classrooms and schools.

> Some objections in this category are based on *professional* considerations. It is argued that politicians, civil servants and inspectors are no more competent to decide on the content and method of what should be taught than the heads and teachers directly responsible. Furthermore, central initiatives and control undermine the partnership between government, local authorities and teachers which offers, on this view, the best view for improving what goes on in classrooms.

> Others object to the *politicisation* of educational decision-making that accompanies an increase in state power at the expense of that of voluntary associations, localities and individuals. It is feared that governments of different persuasions may increasingly succumb to the temptation to use schools to propagate their own values and beliefs.

> There are also those who, whilst prepared to line up with professional arguments against government interventions, take for granted that governments *will* try to influence education for their own ends. Given power themselves, they would do exactly the same. The idea that education should be above politics or teaching should be 'neutral' is treated with scorn. Reference to the national interest is regarded as mere window dressing.

A *second* objection to current policies turns on the *feasibility* of securing improvement by the means proposed. Quality of teaching and organisation and content of syllabuses are seen as much less important in determining educational outcomes than context variables such as social background, race, and regional traditions in such matters as the proportion of qualified 18-year-olds who enter higher education or employment.

> The arguments of those who point to significant differences in outcomes between schools of similar socio-economic composition and tradition, and attribute these to leadership, organisation and teaching quality, are on this view unsupported by the bulk of home and overseas evidence. Most *inter-school* differences are seen as attributable to underlying variables *not* susceptible to improvement by better directed effort and harder work by heads and teachers. To focus effort and attention on matters that are the responsibility of schools and providing authorities, distracts attention from the underlying problems of social, racial and sexual inequality and resource distribution.

11

A *third* objection has to do with weaknesses in conceptualisation. Breadth, balance, relevance and differentiation, which occur prominently in *Better Schools*, have been endlessly debated by philosophers of education, and are highly problematic. To treat them otherwise is to claim agreement where none exists.

> There are anxieties on this score about the prominence given to science and mathematics in discussions of the primary and secondary curriculum. It is recognised that too few pupils have acquired a grasp of scientific and mathematical principles adequate for them to play their part in the life and work of a society increasingly based on scientific knowledge. Nonetheless, an increased technological emphasis can go too far, and threaten development of the analytical, critical and evaluative capacities that are the particular contribution of aesthetic subjects and the humanities to the education of the citizen.

> Utilitarian emphases reflect the prominence given to economic factors in the determination of what should be taught: an implied stress on power, money and status as measures of work and success. Such superficial and chimerical sources of personal satisfaction, it is argued, conflict with the pursuit of intellectual and aesthetic activities for their own sake, and deny the intrinsic value of knowledge, understanding and skill.

A *fourth* concern is that central initiatives, especially if they result in more explicit curricula prescriptions (whether developed nationally, locally, at school or even departmental level) will lead teachers to operate according to the lowest common denominator. Risks will be avoided, individuality stifled, worthwhile change inhibited. A stress on assessment in all its forms may lead teachers to bother only with what contributes directly to pupil credentials or the advancement of their own careers.

Fifth, there are worries about the prominence of a subject-oriented approach to the organisation of knowledge and design of curricula.

> Many teachers find it helpful to think in terms of areas of experience, of subject groupings, of generic skills. The subject-based curriculum is seen as insufficiently related to the way in which knowledge is acquired and used in the contemporary world: conservative in its pedagogic implications and likely to fragment and deny coherence to students' experience of schooling. Subject-trained teachers will want to teach subjects. Previous attempts to redraw the maps of knowledge by pulling together distinctive contributions from several specialisms have not proved successful. To develop an integrated, issue-oriented, interdisciplinary curriculum requires teachers to have experienced a similar mode of higher education and training.

We will each of us have our own response to criticisms such as these. On the challenge to government intervention represented by the first of them, it is mistaken to identify what *Better Schools* has to say about evaluation and appraisal with the political philosophy of a single government. It also gives false comfort to those who hope that when governments change such concerns change with them. They don't. Any policy for improvement worthy of the name has to have more than a five-year (or even ten-year) time horizon.

Nor should arguments about the relative influence of in-school and beyond-school factors blind us to the fact that for very many individuals — including many at this conference — the quality of learning opportunities experienced, the kind of help and advice received, has made a crucial difference to their subsequent life chances.

The problematics of many of the terms we use in educational debate and in the statement of policy are real enough. It is unsurprising, however, that in response to the pluralism of institutional structure and authority, to the increasing opacity of the language of educational discussion, and to the problems of single-interest politics which currently bedevil democratic societies, attempts to state broad cross-curricular objectives in simpler terms have struck a sympathetic chord. To take an example from a distant shore, the Director of Education for New Zealand has defined the curricular basics with admirable clarity:

> 'There is...considerable agreement about what people have in mind when they talk about the basics. The basics that are referred to are a mixture of abilities, understandings and dispositions. The abilities include communicating effectively in speaking and writing, listening and reading with understanding, and basic numeracy. The understandings include some understanding of the kind of world we live in, of New Zealand society, of the responsibilities of citizens, and of the world of work. The dispositions we are talking about are honesty, dependability, initiative, self-discipline, adaptability, being able to get on with others, and above all, an openness to new experience which shows an ability to go on learning'.

With their distaste for intellectuality, the British have never been wholly happy about discussion of the aims, purposes, objectives and tasks of education. Talking about education smacks of the pulpit: all right in small doses on Sundays or in-service courses but without much connection with the every-day effort of doing good in classrooms. And even when aims and purposes and objectives and tasks *do* have to be talked about, better it be done indirectly, obliquely, on Pope's principle:

> Men must be taught as if you taught them not
> and things unknown proposed as things forgot.

Reluctance on the part of some to essay direct statements about educational purposes and teachers' tasks is based on something deeper than cultural habit and aesthetic preference. It reflects a belief that, as in the case of other arts, to describe teaching directly is to trivialise it —

13

to suggest that good practice can be reduced to a series of relatively simple prescriptions.

Such resistance to making aims and tasks explicit also indicates anxieties that the next step from one person adumbrating a comprehensive list of tasks is for it to be imposed as professional imperative or job description.

The individuals most effective in getting things done in schools are not always those who articulate their aims most readily, who construct complex decision-trees, spray self-evaluation questionnaires around the staffroom, and use the latest eduspeak in the frequent lunchtime and after-school workshops and meetings in which they seek to involve colleagues. Such behaviour reminds teachers of someone's cynical remark that what matters in this world is not what you do, but what you say you are going to do and what you claim you've done.

Yet to look back to a golden age when the closed classroom door ensured to Scale 1 neophyte and Mr Chips[1] alike the same protection, and every teacher taught according to his lights, is to forget that absence of talk about aims did not mean that they were absent. Wisely or not, agreement about the nature of the school's task and the teacher's task was assumed. No need, therefore, for the time-consuming complications of discussion and consultation.

If such an attitude was ever appropriate, it is not so today. For individual students and their families as much as for state, economy and society, the effectiveness of learning and teaching matters too much to be left to chance. Despite right-wing jeremiads and left-wing critics with a vested interest in dissent, our culture has for the most part successfully sustained adherence to, and personal behaviour and social practice based upon, certain core values. And although in a democratic society with a social history such as our own there is inevitably an adversarial element in the discussion of aims and purposes (particularly in their media presentation), it would be wrong not to note the common elements to be found in, for example, the Hargreaves report[2], *Better Schools*, the Schools Council's *Practical Curriculum*[3, 4] and many local authority documents setting out policies for school improvement. Those who object to the Government having a view on the curriculum; those who argue that outcomes are determined by variables outside the control of the teacher and the

---

[1] Central character in J Hilton's novel *Goodbye Mr Chips*.

[2] Inner London Education Authority. *Improving Secondary Schools*. Report of the Committee on the Curriculum and Organisation of Secondary Schools, chaired by David H Hargreaves. London: ILEA, 1984.

[3] Schools Council. *The Practical Curriculum*. (Schools Council Working Paper No. 70). London: Methuen Educational, 1981.

[4] Schools Council. *Planning One-Year 16–17 Courses*. A follow up to *The Practical Curriculum*. London: 1983 (Schools Council Pamphlet No. 21) (Now only available as a microfiche from Chadwyck Healey).

school; those who dislike the language that other speakers use on the subject; those who fear that identifying particular objectives will limit effort to those objectives; those who are anxious that reference to traditional subjects will ossify the curriculum, whether they are parents, teachers, academics or administrators, still share a large number of assumptions about what pupils of a given age should be taught and should learn. And fortunately, there are now plenty of examples of schools and colleges where institutional self-study and evaluation, a high level of collegial involvement in the discussion of both long-term and short-run objectives, more conscious accountability, and a clearer focus on outcomes have developed without recourse to jargon, to an excessive load of meetings, to severe loss of school and teacher autonomy, or the bureaucratisation and routinisation that can accompany efforts to make objectives, process and outcomes more conscious and explicit.

Achieving improvement

But do we know what makes for effective teaching and learning? Many hundreds of studies have been undertaken on the kinds of teaching that make for pupil gains in mathematical, linguistic and other forms of cognitive knowledge and understanding; a somewhat smaller number on a variety of non-cognitive variables. Experimental designs have ranged from large-scale presage-process-product surveys to detailed ethnographic studies of individual teachers and classrooms.

In social science research neological inventiveness attracts more attention and status than careful replication. The resulting plethora of models and conceptual schemes makes it imprudent to claim that all the research tells the same story, although there is an impressive measure of agreement.

Let me offer a few examples based mainly on work done in the United States and in England and Wales.

Purkey and Smith (1983)[1] review a hundred or so research reports in the context of a model of *school culture*:

> 'School culture perspective rejects the view that schools are relatively static constructs of discrete variables. Instead schools are thought to be dynamic social systems made up of interrelated factors... This mix of interconnected characteristics is unique to each school and provides each with a definite personality or climate'.

Their approach is attractive because it coincides with the emphasis that parents and prospective members of staff adopt when they have opportunity to have a choice of school—holistic and impressionistic rather than focused on one or two outstanding features. (Miss X may

---

[1] Purkey S C and Smith M S (1983). 'Effective Schools: a review'. *Elementary School Journal* 83:4.

be marvellous at getting reading results, but who's to say that Johnny
will have Miss X as his teacher? Their A-level results are outstanding
— but at what price? — and so on.) Effectiveness requires the right
mix, not just the right ingredients.

Nine school-level structural and organisational factors are identified by
Purkey and Smith as having been supported by existing research:

i *Adequate autonomy for principal and staff to devise their own paths to
improvement*

Traditionally this has not been a problem in this country, where heads
and teachers have been free to determine their objectives and how they
will be achieved. But something to be remembered, especially in the
context of proposals for the determination of the school's curricular aims
and objectives by the governing body, and the political basis on which
appointments to such bodies are sometimes made.

ii *Educational leadership*

Recent years have seen a renewed interest in the quality of leadership in
schools. *Better Schools* emphasises that all new heads should be: 'carefully
selected, inducted, trained and systematically supported in their new
duties' (para 184). These include responsibility for the 'organisation and
delivery of the curriculum' (para 232).

It is important to emphasise it is *educational* leadership we are talking
about, not just administrative and organisational skill. There is evidence
from many types of educational institution — including universities —
that the commitment of the head to educational aims and purposes, not
just his or her ability to see that the accounts are in order and the forms
duly completed, is what really counts.

iii *Staff stability*

Only a few years ago primary heads were raising eyebrows on in-service
courses and in the columns of the *Times Educational Supplement* with tales
of starting the school year with a staff consisting wholly or mainly of
probationers. Not so today. Falling rolls have radically changed the
scene; the problem now is to maintain motivation and morale among a
teaching force that faces diminished mobility and opportunities for
promotion within and beyond the school.

Such evidence as we have on the effects of experience indicates
differences in effectiveness between teachers with less and with more
than five years in the classroom respectively, but little significant
difference beyond the five-year point.

iv *Careful curriculum planning and implementation*

Year and subject syllabuses are not enough. There has to be a
comprehensive design for the whole curriculum, which takes into account
prior experience, makes explicit provision for progression from one stage

to the next, embodies appropriate criteria for evaluation, and reckons with where students will go and what they are likely to be called upon to do beyond school. Such a curriculum identifies the forms of understanding, the skills and the dispositions into which students will be initiated through their subject studies; year and subject syllabuses, and teachers' individual schemes of work should correspond with this broader context.

At all levels of education, up to and including the university, there is a greater emphasis today on requirements, on core studies, on coherence than a few years ago, when smorgasbord principles were more in evidence.

v *Staff development*

The evidence suggests that staff development programmes aid effectiveness when closely related to the school's instructional programme, supported and reinforced at the highest levels; when they reflect teachers' informed perceptions of their own needs; and when all staff are involved, not just those who need the experience either as a basis for promotion or as a last ditch effort at remediation.

Better induction and better INSET has been the received wisdom for at least the past 15 years. The money now being made available for extending INSET opportunities is greatly to be welcomed. As far as induction is concerned, there is still a long way to go before the aspirations of a decade and more ago are achieved.

Reid (1984)[1] showed that only two-fifths of his sample of PGCE-trained probationers had special arrangements made for them by their schools in their first year. They reported their major problems were having to teach subjects for which they had not been prepared by their training; coping with marking; lack of non-teaching time; the preparation of lessons; difficulty in controlling individual pupils and whole classes; dealing with the administrative tasks associated with teaching; inadequate text-books and audio-visual aids and lack of direction from established staff — all matters on which a carefully planned induction programme might have been helpful.

vi *Parental involvement and support*

Evidence on the relation of such support to overall effectiveness is mixed — more so than in the case of some other variables. Perhaps this reflects the varied socio-economic environments in which schools operate, with their different traditions of parental interest and involvement.

---

[1] Reid K (1984). 'The Probationary Year: Facts, Fallacies, Research and the Practical Implications'. *CORE* 8:2.

Better Schools builds on the measures enacted in the 1980 Education Act and proposed mandatory annual reports to parents and a full meeting at least annually (para 250).

vii *Recognition of academic success on a school-wide basis*

Here we are on controversial ground. The authors of the research review, headings from which I have employed in this part of my talk, are quite clear that —

'A school's culture is partially reflected in its ceremonies, its symbols, and the accomplishments it chooses to recognise officially. Schools that make a point of publicly honouring academic achievement and stressing its importance through appropriate use of symbols, ceremonies and the like, encourage students to adopt similar norms and values' (Purkey and Smith 1983, p 444).

In the past, some heads and teachers have had mixed feelings about explicit recognition of academic achievement in this way. Valuing the potential contribution of each child, however limited his or her academic achievement, has suggested to some that the accomplishments of the gifted are their own reward. In tune with the spirit of our times, there is perhaps greater willingness today to use an element of competition at school level, tempered by some broadening of the criteria of success and of the range of accomplishments at which students can realistically aim.

Americans have always felt easier in the face of competition than we in this country, although it was an American (Gardner (1961)) who wrote:

'. . .extreme emphasis on performance as a criterion of status may foster an atmosphere of raw striving that results in brutal treatment of the less able, or less vigorous, or less aggressive; it may wantonly injure those whose temperament or whose values make them unwilling to engage in performance rivalries; it may penalize those whose undeniable excellences do not add up to the kinds of performance that society at any given moment chooses to reward' (p 18).

Gardner's book was called *Excellence; can we be equal and excellent too?* He came to the conclusion that we could. To do so, however, without incurring the social penalities of failure for the majority, required that excellence be sought in every area of life, that it be recognised that anyone who does a slovenly job 'whether he is janitor or a judge, a surgeon or a technician — lowers the tone of the society'.

viii *Maximised learning time*

Here we come to an aspect of the research literature to which I want to return when I come to discuss classroom variables. Sufficient to say that at school level the evidence supports maximising what has been called 'academic engaged time' at the expense of other activities that are peripheral to (or sometimes inhibit) learning.

ix *Local authority support*

Purkey and Smith contend that 'Few, if any, of the variables found to be significant are likely to be realised without district support'. I imagine few heads or chief education officers in this country would disagree.

Having identified these nine structural and organisational correlates of effectiveness at school level, Purkey and Smith suggest there are four important *process* variables which sustain a productive school culture:

i collaborative planning and collegial relationships;

ii a strong sense of community;

iii shared and clearly stated goals and expectations; and

iv 'clear, reasonable rules, fairly and consistently enforced'.

The importance of school culture is its emphasis on wholes rather than parts. As Mackenzie (1983)[1] has put it,

> 'When effective schools are examined *in vivo*, what emerges is not a checklist of specific ingredients but a "syndrome" or "culture" of mutually reinforcing expectations and activities' (p 8.)

Classroom variables

The volume of research on school-level variables that influence effectiveness is matched, or even exceeded, by that on classroom factors. What *does* make for better teaching? It helps to know, even if we are still left with the problem of how best practice is made more general and consistent.

Several things are obvious from the start. Teaching is an art, not a technology. Detailed study and analysis, however careful, cannot generate comprehensive and situationally specific procedural rules which teachers can learn and then apply in order consistently to obtain a desired outcome. There is no single route to classroom effectiveness. Teachers know this. It is one of the reasons that makes them wary of proposals for evaluation and appraisal which do not recognise the complexity of the teaching/learning relationship. It is here that detailed studies in the ethnographic tradition of how teachers work have been so valuable.

Regularities revealed by even the most carefully designed survey cannot of their nature do justice to the uniqueness of each successful teacher's art. This does not mean that lists of effective practices derived from surveys are useless. But we have to recognise that such schedules are in themselves only of *limited* use; it is only when

---

[1] Mackenzie D E (1983). 'Research for School Improvement: an appraisal of some recent trends'. *Educational Researcher*, April.

translated into coherent programmes of initial and in-service training and experience, mediated by skilled and sensitive practitioners through precept, principle and practice, that they begin to influence what you and I do in classroom, laboratory, lecture room or administrative office.

One set of classroom variables that receives a lot of attention in the literature is the quality of teachers' management and organisation for learning. One early study, much quoted in subsequent reviews, (Brophy 1979, 1983)[1, 2] identifies five characteristics of effective classroom management behaviour.

First, 'withitness' — awareness of what is going on everywhere in the classroom, being able to interpret and act upon the meaning of verbal and visual cues.

Second, 'overlapping' — the ability to handle a number of different tasks simultaneously without, as it were, the edges showing.

Third, momentum and pacing — pursuing the objects of a lesson in a brisk but smooth manner, taking potentially disruptive interruptions in one's stride.

Fourth, maintaining a high level of group alertness and accountability — by random questioning, and by keeping students 'attentive to presentations because something new or exciting could happen at any time, and to keep them accountable for learning the content by making them aware that they might be called on at any time'.

Finally, variety and challenge in what Americans call 'seatwork'. Much work has been done on this last point. It has produced interesting findings about the success rate that students need to achieve in order to maintain motivation and understanding when working individually. Success rates of 70–80 per cent are effective when a teacher is present to provide immediate feedback and to monitor responses. But in the case of homework and individual assignments, higher rates are needed if progress is to be maintained. Much more massive reinforcement of success is required than intuition indicates. Thus teachers' choice of questions and material in relation to the ability and responses of particular groups and individuals can be crucial to subsequent success. All this has implications for the quality of initial and in-service training.

---

[1] Brophy J E (1979). 'Teacher Behaviour and its Effects'. *Journal of Educational Psychology* 71:6.
[2] Brophy J E (1983). 'Classroom Organisation and Management'. *The Elementary School Journal* 83:4.

In writing about these matters Gage (1984)[1] refers not to the *science* of teaching, but the *scientific basis of the art of teaching*. He says:

'If teaching is an art in large degree, it cannot be taught in the same way that we use to train assembly-line workers, aircraft mechanics, or medical technicians. Teachers need more autonomy and more freedom to use their judgement than any workers of that kind. But teaching is an art with obligations to the society, with moral imperatives relating to the welfare of students and the body politic. So teachers cannot have the complete autonomy of the creative artist who can choose to be a surrealist, an atonalist, or a dadaist. Thus we need approaches to teacher education that will walk the path between unacceptable regimentation and unacceptable anarchy'.

Classifying teaching styles

A lesson learned from studies of teaching styles is the difficulty of categorising teaching behaviour in terms such as progressive, traditional or formal. Some recent work on teaching styles, about to be published in a report from the National Foundation for Educational Research (NFER), and involving both longitudinal and cross-sectional studies, supports earlier findings that, depending upon circumstances, class teaching, group work and individualised approaches can all be equally successful (see Boydell 1980)[2]. The NFER researchers show that within particular teaching styles there are a number of specific characteristics and practices which make for less or more effective teaching. These they classify under the headings of discipline and control, classroom organisation and management, and instructional technique.

Aspects of instructional technique that made for success were: giving clear instructions and checking they had been understood; achieving an appropriate balance between instruction and classwork (in which connection an interesting non-linear relationship between academic interaction and pupil performance was shown); striking a balance between whole class teaching and attending to individual pupils; skilful use of questioning for purposes of recapitulation, to check that instructions have been understood, for exposition and to maintain order; and the application of immediate feedback—not only prompt marking, but also 'public praise and private criticism'.

The longitudinal aspect of the NFER study complicates the issue of style by suggesting that consistency in teacher effectiveness and teacher performance over two successive years was only 'moderate'. Much depends on the setting. Before any particular style can be recommended as 'effective' there needs to be a full appraisal of the nature and requirements of the subjects to be taught and of student

---

[1] Gage N (1984). *Hard Gains in the Soft Sciences: The Case of Pedagogy*. Bloomington, Ind: *Phi Delta Kappan*.

[2] Boydell D (1980). 'The Organisation of Junior School Classrooms: a follow up survey'. *Educational Research* 23:1, November.

characteristics, as well as of the attributes and preferences, strengths and weaknesses of teachers themselves.

As emphasised earlier, there is no simple technology of teaching. Teachers have to be flexible enough to adapt methods and styles to circumstances generated by the interaction between the characteristics of particular student groups and what it is intended should be acquired by way of information, understanding and skill. We are back to the need for a holistic approach. Comprehensive analyses of the teacher's task, thorough disaggregation of the elements that enter into particular teaching performances, and efforts to relate these to outcomes can all be valuable, especially in offering a more systematic structure for the professional aspects of initial training and INSET. Teachers need, however, the confidence, perceptiveness and flexibility that enable them to respond to circumstances that vary not just from year to year, but from day to day and period to period.

Active learning time

One classroom variable with consistent positive relationships with achievement is the *time* available and used for learning. Studies have been made of the formal length of the school year, the school day and subject allocated time in relation to outcomes. Others have looked in somewhat more detail at students' actual involvement in instruction, as measured by attendance and engagement in learning activities. A number of studies have employed the measure of 'time on task', ie., the amount of time an average student is actively engaged in or attending to academic instruction or tasks. (Caldwell *et al* 1982)[1]. Researchers have refined this measure as 'academic learning time', the amount of time a student spends attending to relevant academic tasks *while performing with a high rate of success*. Such a measure takes into account findings referred to earlier on rates of success needed to ensure progress. Academic learning time has been found to be strongly associated with achievement. All this makes it important that time available for learning is used to the full, and distribution of teacher and student effort during available time is such as to maximise 'time on task' and 'academic learning time' (Leach and Tunnicliffe 1984)[2].

Some years ago, the NFER reported on studies of how primary and secondary teachers spend their day. Forty-three per cent of the teaching session time available to primary teachers was used for actual lesson instruction to a class, a group or an individual pupil. The corresponding figure for secondary teachers was 33 per cent. A further 16 per cent of primary teachers' time and 12 per cent of their secondary counterparts' time went on organising pupils, and the

[1]Caldwell H J, Huitt W G and Graeber, A O (1982). 'Time Spent in Learning; implications from research', *The Elementary School Journal* 82: 5.
[2]Leach D J and Tunnicliffe M R (1984). 'The Relative Influence of Time Variables on Primary Mathematics Achievement'. *Australian Journal of Education* 28:2.

remainder on a variety of other tasks, including supervision, mechanical chores, lesson planning and so on.

Given the general tendency for time-related variables to correlate significantly with achievement, sharp variations in 'academic learning time' between schools and teachers, and over time in the same school and with the same teacher, are matters of some concern. Hilsum and Strong (1978)[1,2] found large variations across the period of their study in the time devoted to various activities. In a single day, the amount of direct teaching undertaken might vary from $1\frac{1}{2}$ to $3\frac{1}{4}$ hours. US studies report time actually allocated for second-grade mathematics ranging from 24 minutes at one extreme to 61 minutes at another, and for second grade reading from 32 minutes to 131 minutes. This research has also shown considerable variations within classes on the amount of time that individual pupils spend on a particular subject— an example is quoted of a fifth-grade student spending 39 minutes on maths, while another in the same class spent 75 minutes (Caldwell *et al* 1982)[3].

Praising and blaming

To conclude these few illustrative examples of variables, associated with achievement that have been the subject of systematic research, a word about praise.

Technically, we can regard praise as an aspect of the more general process of feedback. Psychologists have long been concerned with the role of praise in reinforcing behaviour. Some theories of teaching depend heavily on its use for the purposes of motivation and control. We do not have to be behaviourists, however, to recognise the importance of the part played by praise in almost every aspect of social life, including life in classrooms. Whether expressed in terms of the lapel button or teeshirt emblazoned 'Smile!', or in terms of behaviour reinforcement through positive feedback, we all recognise the importance of this aspect of handling relationships among individuals and in groups.

The choice of praise as the last of my examples of classroom variables that have been studied in connection with improving teaching is not, of course, accidental. The feelings aroused by formal appraisal and evaluation procedures are intimately connected with our personal response to praise and to blame. Very few observations we make about the behaviour of others, or which we hear or interpret about our own, are neutral.

---

[1]Hilsum S and Cane B (1971). *The Teacher's Day*. Slough: National Foundation for Educational Research.

[2]Hilsum S and Strong B (1978). *The Secondary Teacher's Day*. Slough: National Foundation for Educational Research.

[3]Caldwell H J, Huitt W G and Graeber, A O (1982). 'Time Spent in Learning; implications from research', *The Elementary School Journal* 82: 5.

According to that combination of nature and nurture that has made us what we are, there is great variation in need for and response to praise. At one end of the spectrum, excessive sensitivity can seriously inhibit action and create crippling anxiety. At the other, indifference to the judgements of others produces behaviour we label psychopathic.

There is no evidence that effective teaching is the prerogative of particular personality types. One reason why appraisal and evaluation need to be undertaken as close as possible to the actual work setting is the need to take fully into account the personality characteristics of those assessed or evaluated. What is water-off-a-duck's-back to one person can be a crushing rebuke to another. To depersonalise appraisal and evaluation is to destroy much of its purpose, but as the Suffolk report[1] emphasises there is need nonetheless to ensure that the assessment dialogue is task-oriented.

Using what we know

The school-effectiveness literature has attracted plenty of criticism. The criteria by which effectiveness is judged are often very narrow, being limited to gains in test scores in English, mathematics and other basic subjects. Only a small number of studies are longitudinal and take account of the possibility of lack of stability from year to year, both in teacher behaviour and pupil characteristics and response, identified in the recent NFER study. Not all the instruments employed in school-effectiveness research have been adequately piloted and validated. There has been a tendency to focus attention on high achieving schools and classes. Not enough studies involve comparison groups. Fuzzy conceptualisation of variables is still commonplace; this has weakened the impact of many studies, including those on time variables. Not enough account is always taken of unreliability of observer ratings of similar events. There is disagreement about the relative merits of class teaching, group work and individualised instruction, even in specific subject areas. Perhaps most serious of all, we do not know enough about how the many variables interact together to create an overall climate or culture conducive to effectiveness.

All these criticisms are familiar enough to those working in the field, and efforts continue to improve the reliability and validity of instruments and measures and the significance of findings. But the weaknesses of some existing research do not justify neglect of what *has* been found out. Nor should they deter us from attempting to incorporate useful findings into our policies for school improvement.

But how? Obviously not by expecting every individual teacher to be familiar with the relevant research. A large gap still exists between the

---

[1]Suffolk Education Department (1985). *Those Having Torches*: *Teacher Appraisal*. A study funded by the DES. Ipswich: the Education Department. (See also paper 4.1.)

printed page of the research journal and the day-to-day life of classrooms.

Many attempts have been made to summarise what we know from research on school-effectiveness in a series of relatively straightforward propositions. For example, Guzzetti (1983)[1] suggests that such research shows effective schools to be strongly goal-oriented, both at school and classroom level; teachers in such schools undertake systematic diagnosis of pupil needs, and progress and modify and adapt their materials to recognise these; both formal and informal measures for evaluation and assessment are regularly employed; teaching methods are eclectic, involving a mixture of whole class, group and individual teaching, according to circumstances, to ensure that every member of the class is actively involved in learning (not always the case, as Simon and his associates showed, when the emphasis is on one-to-one teaching). In effective schools, too, effectively engaged time, which I have called elsewhere in this paper academic learning time, constitutes a high proportion of all the available time; a climate exists that encourages high expectations by both teachers and students, and which is safe and orderly; evidence of student work, especially in primary schools, is prominently displayed; principals are strong instructional leaders, and involved in classroom work; there are high levels of parent-initiated involvement; and, finally, staff are dissatisfied people, not content to maintain existing practices but actively in search of new ideas and techniques, interacting frequently with each other for this purpose.

I argued at the beginning of this paper that we know a good deal about what makes for better schools. Adding to and refining knowledge is unlikely to be helpful unless we have means of turning such knowledge into good practice. And this, of course, is where improved initial training and induction, INSET, and a high level of professionalism within the individual school all come into play. Ultimately, the responsibility is that of the individual teacher, working as a member of a departmental or school team, conscious through stringent self-evaluation and agreed procedures for external appraisal of strengths and weaknesses, knowing where help in solving problems is to be found and willing to seek it out, able to offer specialist assistance (and not just in terms of subject) to other colleagues, and enjoying that progressively greater measure of personal satisfaction that comes from student achievement and the sense of working in an institution that is well-led, knows where it is going, and is able to support and sustain its members.

There is a certain cultural reticence about the satisfactions and the joys of teaching. Their over-elaboration can indeed trivialise the

---

[1]Guzzetti B J (1983). 'A Critical Synthesis of School-Effectiveness Research: Implications for Dissemination'. Paper presented to the Northern Rocky Mountain American Educational Research Association, Jackson Hole, Wyoming (mimeo).

teaching/learning relationship. But if some sense of dignity is to be restored to the art and practice of teaching, new initiatives are necessary. Some have seen these as including efforts to establish teaching on a more professional basis, perhaps by the creation of a General Teachers' Council or some other national professional body. With or without such a body, the more systematic forms of evaluation and appraisal that are the subject of this conference need to be consistent with a genuine professionalism. And in initial training as in INSET, we need what CI Mrs Pauline Perry has elsewhere called a more 'rigorous pedagogy' which gives full weight to research of the kind mentioned in this paper.

It is the responsibility of the Secretary of State and of local authorities to provide the framework within which better schools can be created. But it is the task of the profession to accept responsibility for improvement where it really counts—in the school and the individual classroom. It is *this* which is today among the most important tasks of the school and of the teacher.

Assessment Techniques and Approaches

2.0 An Overview

Eric J Bolton, Senior Chief Inspector, HM Inspectorate

There is, I imagine, little disagreement with the general idea that the work of the education system should be subject to a range of assessments, evaluations and reviews. But every particular attempt to introduce or reform an assessment or evaluation procedure seems to give rise to prolonged, and sometimes bitter, debate and argument.

Public examinations are perhaps the most obvious example from the last 20 years. Some would of course argue for their total abolition, but even those who take that view would in general substitute some other way of assessing pupils' performance. Each proposal for change has rightly been subjected to critical scrutiny because there genuinely are dangers. We know from experience that examinations can be designed or used so that they limit pupils' development; so that they favour this or that section of society; so that they lead to rigidity in the system, preventing change and development; so that they exercise an undesirable and over-strong influence on what is taught. The current debates about the appraisal of the performance of teachers and the evaluation and assessment of whole schools reveal sharply divided views about the efficiency of proposed techniques, and rightly stress the complexity of the realities with which these techniques seek to deal. Yet judgements are frequently made about individual teachers and particular schools—judgements which often have a significant effect for the futures of those concerned, and few people can be satisfied that such judgements are usually soundly based. What is at issue is not whether judgements should or will be made—the question is how are they going to be made.

Indeed, a national education system costing over £13 billion, having as its central purpose the education of the people of England and Wales, that was not subject to review, evaluation and assessment is unthinkable. In one way or another, of course, a great deal of assessment and evaluation takes place all the time, nationally, at LEA level and in schools and classrooms. Some of this—public examinations for example—is carried out across the whole country. Whereas much of the rest is local (LEA screening programmes, for example), or confined to individual schools or even to particular parts of a school.

Whatever the real or perceived limitations of performance assessments of one kind of another, the fact is that in our school system those assessments that enable general messages to be discerned and comparisons to be made across all or large parts of it, are in exceedingly short supply. In some other European countries, which appear to have fewer tests and seem to make less use of external examinations, there is greater national or regional agreement about the curriculum and about the standards to be achieved by the full range of pupils. Within these frameworks the teachers are entrusted with the important tasks of assessment carried out at various stages of the pupils' educational careers. We do not have such frameworks favouring and facilitating assessment. Moreover, certainly at secondary school level, we appear to have more complex objectives for our schools and consequently ask more of our teachers across the gamut of academic, social and personal aims and objectives.

Much of the same lack of helpful and useful data about the performance of various parts of the system exists at LEA level, although quite a number of authorities have developed systems for screening pupil performance. Although these screening programmes differ from authority to authority, in the main they deal with little more than reading, numeracy and verbal reasoning. In these screening programmes, most LEAs make use of one or other of the variously standardised tests available, none of which is free from controversy as to their reliability, relevance and usefulness in the situations in which they are used.

In schools much assessment is for specific purposes and it is thus not standardised in any way. Nonetheless, there is an understandable and perfectly respectable case for wishing to know how the performance of schools in similar and different circumstances compares. That is not only of interest and use to those outside the schools, such as the LEAs and parents, but it is, or should be, of great importance to the school itself. Any half-way-good school needs and wants to know how it is performing, and part of the answer to that question involves a comparison, however crude, with similar schools in similar circumstances as well as with schools of the same general type in different circumstances.

Perhaps more pressingly in need of consistent assessment and review inside schools is what has come to be called 'the value added factor': what has the teaching and learning in the school added to the pupils' competence, understanding, knowledge and skills? To assess the 'value added' calls for not only suitable instruments and techniques, but also some way of knowing where the pupils started from and where they got to if we are to judge whether the journey was worthwhile. To somewhat oversimplify this complex matter if may be helpful to view it as having two broad uses:

    a. as an input/output model;

b. as a means of allowing for the effects that external social background factors have on performance.

At the levels of the individual teacher and school it is important to be able to gauge what has been achieved by the pupils in the light of some understanding of where they started from and of what they are capable, and to recognise that even relatively good performance may be poor for those pupils, and indicate poor teaching. This is generally important for all pupils in any type of school. But it is crucial in schools where, despite the best efforts of the teachers, the performance of the pupils as a group falls far short of what can be generally expected of the age range. However, while an assessment of the value added by schools may show that relatively low or poor performance is not a function of poor teaching, it is essential that sight is not lost of the fact that by national standards the performance is poor. Keeping both perspectives in a constructive balance lies at the heart of the difficult task that faces many teachers of maintaining high expectations of individual pupils, while knowing that affecting their pupils generally are realities external to the schools, inimical to educational success and only marginally influenced by good schools and effective teaching.

Both LEAs and the Government must also take account of these external factors that act to depress performance. Without measures which help them to do this there is a danger that the efforts and quality of many teachers and schools will be seriously underestimated; that the success of others will be as seriously overestimated; that morale in schools serving difficult catchment areas will be adversely affected; and, more generally, that we will not achieve clarity about which 'in-school' factors do influence performance in all circumstances and risk misdirecting our priorities for raising standards throughout the system. Some work has been done in this difficult area including Professor Rutter's study that culminated in *Fifteen Thousand Hours*[1], that of the National Council for Educational Standards (NCES); John Grey initially in Edinburgh and now in Sheffield; David Reynolds' work in South Wales and Peter Mortimore's in the ILEA. At national level the DES's Statistical Branch has developed ways in which social and economic background factors can be allowed for when appraising the relative examination performance of secondary schools in particular LEAs. But this work tells us little about the performance of individual schools and how that is affected by in-school and out-of-school factors. The Secretary of State has invited proposals for further research in this controversial area that focuses upon the individual school and develops more effective and wide-ranging measures of school performance.

---

[1]Rutter, Michael. *Fifteen Thousand Hours: Secondary Schools and their Effects on Children.* Shepton Mallet, Somerset: Open Books, 1979.

In seeking to be better informed about the performance of schools and progress towards desired ends there are differences of degree, emphasis and detail between what the Government, the LEAs, schools and individual teachers need to know. But generally in evaluating and appraising the performance of schools and teachers we are all, in one way or another, concerned with:

i. the curriculum that is offered: its coverage, structure and relevance in terms of what is available to pupils generally as well as what each individual pupil receives;

ii. the quality of teaching, and of other education processes and learning experiences provided for pupils across the whole curriculum and the whole period of their school education;

iii. the standards achieved by pupils in relation to their abilities, aptitudes and circumstances across the whole curriculum and period of schooling.

In part assessing what is offered through the curriculum in terms of coverage is a descriptive business. All secondary schools set out the curriculum offered in one form or another and, despite the decentralised nature of our education system, there is a high degree of curricular similarity across all maintained secondary schools in what is offered to pupils. Where such common ground begins to run out is in what each individual secondary pupil receives, particularly after the age of 13 when option systems become operative. Thus, while most schools may have overall curricular provision that is both broad and balanced, the curricular programme of individual pupils may be both narrow and unbalanced. To some extent this disparity between all that is offered by a school and what constitutes the curricular programmes of individual pupils arises from the growth, historically, of what is generally believed should be provided via the school curriculum. Secondary schools have attempted to respond to new and changing expectations as well as maintaining much of what might be termed 'traditional provision'. Clearly there should be, in many schools, somewhat different and better guidance for pupils and their parents and a greater element of constraint at the point when options come into play, and perhaps there should be less unguided choice available. But secondary schools do have a quarts-into-pint-pots problem, and while they can, by and large, provide whatever they think they should provide somewhere within the curriculum, they cannot provide it all, in the same way, for every pupil.

In addition to questions of curricular provision and coverage schools have to respond to the call by *Better Schools* for 'relevance' and 'differentiation' within the curriculum. To some degree relevance relates to overall provision: to resolve the quarts-into-pint-pots problem, some priorities must be determined. Deciding what must be there for all throughout the whole 5–16 period and what needs to be there for some pupils but not for others; for some of the time for all and for all of the time for others, are to some extent conditioned by notions of relevance. But 'relevance' of what is taught and learned is much more a questioning of what happens within subjects and areas of the curriculum than it is about overarching curricular coverage. Science for all up to the age of 16 may not be seriously questioned by anyone, but that it should be the same science for all would not be so readily agreed. Equally relevance to whom or what are important questions not open to simple or generally agreed answers. Indeed, 'differentiation' within the curriculum may well be a sub-set of the question 'What kind of maths, science etc for all?' as well as of the question about who should study what. But differentiation also relates to that which pupils of different abilities are able to cope with and to master. That is a much more difficult and contentious matter. Precisely how individual schools cater for pupils of different levels of ability in this or that area of work within a broad, balanced, common curriculum is for individual schools to decide. But it is important that the bases upon which pupils' ability are measured are as sound as possible and that action that follows such individual assessments does not effectively cut pupils off from important areas of study.

Much of what I have just said relates mainly to secondary schools, as indeed does much of the curriculum debate of the last two decades or so. While primary schools must also satisfy themselves and others that their curricula are broad, balanced, relevant and that there is appropriate differentiation, it is by no means clear what kind of curricular model or models should form the basis for review and scrutiny at primary level. Similarly the question of what individual pupils receive is a different kind of question in relation to primary schools, where class teaching is the dominant mode of delivery, from what it is, and implies, when asked of secondary schools. In addition, while external examinations in secondary schools may be agreed by all to be an insufficient measure of the range of pupil performance and school effectiveness, at least they provide some guidance and may be developed so as to do so more effectively. But there are no comparable or different instruments available for obtaining an overall picture of the achievements of primary-aged pupils. There is little to be gained from looking back to the 11-plus, as that was essentially an instrument of selection and not of performance assessment and it often unduly restricted breadth. I will return to the primary phase later. Suffice it to register now that in some ways the challenges raised by evaluating and assessing the performance of schools and pupils are more daunting at primary school level than at secondary.

Since the Secretary of State's Sheffield speech to the North of England Education Conference in January 1984 placed the search for national agreement about the 5 to 16 curriculum on the agenda, there have been further developments. The Government's White Paper *Better Schools* sets out the issues to be faced and the proposed lines of Government policy and action, while the Inspectorate's 'Curriculum

Matters' series has been launched. That series is intended to stimulate a professional discussion about the 5 to 16 curriculum overall, the objectives of its various parts and about standards to be expected at different ages of the broad mass of pupils. That discussion is now well under way following the publication of *The Curriculum from 5 to 16*[1]; English, mathematics, music and home economics and more subjects and curricular areas will follow. It is intended that in relation to each separate pamphlet a further public paper will be produced that analyses the responses and points out areas of broad agreement, of uncertainty and of sharp polarisation of view.

The 'Better Schools' conference was in itself a development of the debate begun in Sheffield in 1984. The papers circulated for this section of the conference are varied in character. Some are related to matters which are highly developed and some to things that are at an early stage: some deal with issues that are firmly part of Government policy, whereas others do not. Three of these (examinations, records of achievement and testing) relate directly to the assessment of standards of learning. But they relate also to the curriculum; to what is offered, received and expected. Inspection, teacher appraisal and school evaluation relate most directly to assessing the quality of the education process, but cannot be separated from what is provided in and through the curriculum, or the assessment of the standards of learning achieved by pupils. The curriculum must reflect what it is believed pupils of different ages and abilities can achieve and master, as well as what society at large, the Government, teachers, employers and parents would like them to have mastered. Similarly, teaching cannot be adjudged good if, set in context, the standards of learning achieved are poor, or if what is learned and mastered is irrelevant, trivial or of little or no value to the pupils.

The work of the APU is beginning to provide a picture across the whole school system of what particular age groups of pupils can achieve and what they find difficult in certain subjects. Examination results, primarily of significance for individual pupils, are easily assembled at school, LEA or whole country levels and can be useful in each of those contexts. Inspection assesses the standards achieved and the quality of performance *in situ*, and the findings can be assembled to give a national, or local picture in the primary and secondary survey reports. Records of achievement are intended to cover the whole curriculum, and more, in relation to individual pupils, but they will be of little use as a basis for the assessment of wider groupings of pupils. School evaluation and teacher appraisal are not intended to, nor can they, provide objective measures of how individual schools or the school system is performing, even though they make use of such objective measures as exist. These two instruments are mainly of importance for the management of schools, the improvement of

---

[1]DES. *The Curriculum from 5 to 16*. (HMI Curriculum Matters No. 2) HMSO, 1985. (See also Bibliography, p 191.)

performance, the provision and use of in-service training and the effective deployment and promotion of teachers.

Many factors contribute to effective learning but there is widespread agreement that the quality of teaching is crucial. Clearly, high quality teaching requires careful nurturing and support if it is to flourish and be sustained. The Government's White Paper *Teaching Quality*[1] and *Circular 3/84*[2] have established arrangements and criteria intended to bring about improvements to initial teacher training, and the proposed direct grant for in-service education and training aims to improve the availability of high quality INSET and its match with the needs of schools and teachers. But we need to be much clearer about the characteristics of good teachers as well as about the conditions that foster and nourish such teachers. In *Education Observed 3: Good Teachers*[3] we drew together from inspection reports what the HMI conducting those inspections appear to regard as the features of good teachers. In that publication and in *Quality in Schools: Evaluation and Appraisal*[4] the Inspectorate is in little doubt about the potential value of effective teacher appraisal. Accepting that appraisal may serve many different purposes, performance in the classroom; the teacher's role in relation to the aims of the school as a whole; and a recognition of personal and professional strengths and weaknesses appear to be essential components. In addition, the appraisal of individual teachers should be set in a positive context, in which LEAs and the senior management of schools have clear staff development policies and programmes that include the availability of effective and appropriate INSET and career development, and being fully aware of those managerial, resource and organisational matters that impinge for good or ill upon the quality of individual teacher performance. At present other matters are preventing debate about the appraisal of the performance of teachers. But sooner or later the professional matters that lie at the heart of teacher appraisal, and which give rise to a need for it, must be seriously addressed if the professional development of teachers, the quality of teaching, and hence the performance of pupils are to be improved to bring much more of what takes place throughout the school system nearer to the level of the best.

School evaluation, or self-assessment, must by definition be fairly all-embracing. Yet at present it tends to be strong in some areas, particularly in curricular review, but weak in others, such as the observation and assessment of classroom practice and pupil performance. In those respects, as I have already said, many schools and teachers are relatively weak in assessing the value added aspects of teaching and learning and lack instruments for assessing their

---

[1]DES. *Teaching Quality*. HMSO, 1983. (Cmnd. 8836).

[2]*Initial Teacher Training: Approval of Courses*. DES, 1984. (Circular 3/84).

[3]*Education Observed 3: Good Teachers*. A paper by HM Inspectorate. DES, 1985. (See also Bibliography).

[4]DES. *Quality in Schools: Evaluation and Appraisal*. An HMI study. HMSO, 1985.

achievements in relation to any generally accepted norms or standards. Missing from most school self-evaluation schemes are ways and means of taking into account the expectations of education of pupils, parents and employers and others outside education, yet all these have legitimate interests in what schools set out to achieve. Clearly LEAs and their educational advisers have an important part to play in enabling schools to set up comprehensive but workable systems of self-appraisal, and need to make clear by their actions that notice is taken of what is revealed by such evaluation by ensuring that constructive action follows. It is also important to recognise that classroom observation and the assessment of pupil performance within school evaluation come very close to teacher performance appraisal, necessarily so because of the key part played in both by teachers and because, in order to improve either, teachers will often require the support of effective in-service education as well as the tools to do the job.

Many schools are now involved in some form of self-evaluation some of which includes the appraisal of teacher performance and further work on appraisal is planned, supported by an education support grant (ESG) if the various parties involved can agree to it going ahead. In public examinations the work on the GCSE and grade criteria is under way, as are pilot projects for records of achievement. The monitoring tests of the Assessment of Performance Unit (APU) are now well established, and important work is proceeding to extract insights from the APU data and present them in ways that will help all concerned, particularly teachers, to improve the effectiveness of teaching and learning. There is no shortage of tests available for use by LEAs and schools for diagnostic purposes, though not all would be regarded as equally sound and useful. The information and judgements derived from HMI inspection, in all its forms, is made increasingly available through a wide variety of published reports.

All that work is important and progress in each is needed by the schools, LEAs and the Government. But there are dangers to be avoided. It is possible for example that:

   i. the search for ever more refined and effective instruments of assessment becomes so technical and rarified it loses contact with the realities of those most directly involved in providing effective education;

  ii. the fact that no technique or instrument is perfect or foolproof leads to no techniques being generally adopted or to the development of instruments that are so complex and time consuming that they are impractical;

 iii. assessment, evaluation and testing become ends in themselves and lose sight of the desired purposes and aims of education: what can be assessed or tested becomes synonymous with what teachers should teach and pupils should learn and what is to be learned becomes fragmented as a consequence of being built on graded tests or modular approaches.

Each of these is a real danger. The public examination industry could, for example, make such a complex business of grade criteria that the education system loses heart and fails to take the opportunity to establish as much criteria-based assessment as is potentially achievable. Similarly, despite the practical and down-to-earth nature of the recent report by Suffolk LEA (see paper 4.1), the fact that no system of teacher appraisal could ever be perfect could be used to work against the development of realistic and sensible performance appraisal that could be of great benefit to the professional development of individual teachers and to improvement in the performance of schools, teachers and pupils. But the most serious danger is that of the assessment cart getting before the worthwhile-objectives horse.

The key to preventing this from happening and, more positively, to developing patterns of assessment, evaluation, testing and appraisal that together act constructively to improve educational achievements, lies in reaching agreement nationally about the objectives of the curriculum 5–16; about the objectives of its various component parts; and about the broad standards expected to be achieved by pupils at different stages of their educational progress. Without such agreement, and the framework it should provide for the work of all involved in making provision for school education, there exists no firm basis upon which the structures and techniques of assessment and evaluation can be built. If we do not know or agree about where we want to get to, how can it be possible to measure whether we are getting there or not? In order to assess whether or not all schools provide, and all pupils receive, a broad, balanced and relevant curriculum, there needs to be agreement about the shape and content of such a curriculum; to judge whether or not the work of schools and teachers is as effective as it should be, broadly agreed standards to be achieved by most and by some pupils are needed. Without this kind of framework, accepted by all, it is difficult to understand how the outcomes of assessment and evaluation can have a broader meaning beyond the particular situation in which they are used.

As I have indicated earlier there is a good deal of work under way that is seeking to establish agreement about the 5–16 curriculum and to clarify both overall objectives and those of its various parts. But achieving agreement about curricular objectives is not an easy task, and there is unease about the whole process that goes deeper than the concern that the objectives themselves will be difficult to identify in helpfully clear ways. There is, for example, concern that what is easy to measure by tests or examinations may be unduly influential in setting curricular objectives. There is a deeper worry that national agreement about such matters constitutes a significant increase in the central control of what is taught in schools and the direction of provision at LEA level. Yet without some such agreement it is difficult to see how the unacceptably wide variation across the country in both what is offered to pupils and what they achieve can be reduced, or how improved assessment and evaluation could have a sufficiently common basis to carry generally useful messages about improvement and change for what is by law, and ought to be in fact, a national system.

Difficult as reaching agreement about curricular objectives may prove to be, at least the process has begun. But there is much less progress as yet in establishing broad agreement about the standards expected to be achieved by most pupils at, say, ages 11 and 16 across the whole curriculum. At 16-plus the GCSE provides one measure and the new national criteria set out usefully, subject by subject, what in general terms it is expected that pupils will cover, and, consequently, what will be examined. The development of grade criteria and drawing some 90 per cent of pupils into the realm of useful qualifications at 16-plus will, if successful, clarify and take further the establishment of broad agreement about achievements at that age. In addition, records of achievement should provide a wider baseline of recognised individual pupil achievement than is possible through examinations alone. But all this work is mainly, or wholly, directed at the secondary phase. There is far less progress towards these particular aims of *Better Schools* in the primary phase and much less clarity about how progress towards them might be furthered.

In secondary education there is a long history of debate and practice in respect of both the curriculum and examinations. Neither is as true of primary education. It is difficult to identify sufficient common ground, or at least sufficient common language, to begin to discuss the primary curriculum nationally, let alone carry out the kind of scrutiny and development required to establish a primary curricular framework and agreed objectives. At every stage such a necessary debate is complicated by sharply polarised disagreements about process and content; teaching children and teaching subject matter; and the balance between generalist and specialist uses of primary teachers. Unlike the secondary phase, there is relatively little history of a sustained debate about, and scrutiny of, the curriculum in primary schools, and while LEAs are now moving, admittedly somewhat slowly, towards establishing curricula-led staffing in their secondary schools, there is very little evidence of any such notion of the primary curriculum developing to which the staffing of the schools could be linked. Yet, paradoxically, the successes of primary education in broadening provision since the 1950s to include music, art, physical science and craft, design and technology (CDT), as well as revealing the high standards that pupils of 10 and 11 can achieve in these and other areas of the curriculum, have added to the pressure for a clearer articulation of what in practice is meant by a broad, balanced and relevant curriculum for 5–11 year-old pupils. Since there is so much similarity of good practice in many primary schools, it looks as if much of the confusion and disagreement about the primary curriculum is essentially semantic. Unless clear formulations can be developed and agreed, and there is no question of forcing primary schools into a secondary curricular mould, it is hard to envisage a constructive approach being developed to the deployment of primary schoolteaching staff; to the initial and in-service education of primary teachers; and to the assessment of how primary schools perform.

There is even less clarity or agreement about the learning standards to be achieved by pupils at the end of the primary phase. As with the debate about the primary curriculum there is a substantial lobby in the primary world that eschews any attempt to establish broad-based notions of standards to be achieved. Some of that resistance stems from a fear about a 'return to the 11-plus' and the restrictions on teaching, learning and children's educational and personal development that went along with it. But the distrust of achievement objectives goes deeper than that. The setting of any external achievement objectives is seen by some as striking at the heart of child-centred primary education. Yet, despite those reservations, most if not all primary teachers have some notions about what they expect their pupils to achieve, not only in terms of individual needs, but as a necessary basis for successful progress through the education system and into the adult world: a preparation for what comes after. Also, most primary teachers would wish parents to understand how the development of the child, on which they are both engaged, relates to the requirements of the 'real world'. Experienced teachers are aware of how the performance of individuals and particular groups of pupils compares with that of similar pupils elsewhere, or those they taught previously. This being so, the challenge facing the primary phase is to articulate those learning objectives in terms of competencies and understandings to be mastered in ways that meet with broad agreement and do not cause damage to what is now commonly agreed to be effective primary practice across a broad and balanced curriculum.

Where then does this leave us in relation to the development of useful techniques, instruments and strategies for assessment and evaluation across the system? There is a lot of useful work under way as the circulated papers make clear, but a number of key issues remain and there are some difficulties to be resolved:

   i. How is progress towards more efficient and effective ways of assessing curricular provision, the quality of education processes and the standards of learning achieved by pupils to be kept in step with the development of agreed curricular objectives and broad agreement about standards of achievement, so as to avoid particular assessment techniques unduly influencing teaching and learning?

   ii. Much of the work on assessment and evaluation to date is biased towards the secondary phase. We lack broad agreement

37

about how to describe and scrutinise the primary curriculum.
The absence of clarity and agreement about what children
should be capable of at various stages of their primary
education leads to a distinct lack of information about
standards of pupil achievement in individual primary schools,
and a consequent difficulty of establishing any standards of
achievement as a basis for an assessment of performance.

iii. While I hope HMI inspection procedures are now fairly well
understood—certainly their findings are now open to public
scrutiny and criticism—there does not appear to be any
generally understood pattern of LEA procedures for inspection
and reporting. I do not imply by this that LEAs should seek
to model the work of their advisory services on the work of
HMI. For one thing the functions of HMI and local advisers
are very different. But inspection is a varied form of
assessment open to great flexibility. What is appropriate for
HMI reporting nationally may need to be considerably
different at local level. But presumably LEAs need to know
how that which they provide is performing overall, and in
particular how it compares with the performance of the system
nationally. The recently circulated DES/LAA consultative
document helpfully addresses this and other questions about
LEA advisory services.

iv. While work on public examination reform, the APU's
findings and records of achievement is well in hand, that on
school self-assessment and teacher appraisal is patchy and still
at a stage where much more work in the development of
effective and acceptable instruments and techniques is
required.

I have, I know, touched upon the difficulties, problems and areas of
disagreement in relation to assessment and evaluation of schools,
teachers and pupil performance. But it is important to end by saying
that assessment, evaluation, review and testing are, or should be,
concerned with helping to bring about improvements in the education
of pupils. Whatever the real or perceived dangers and risks, external
examinations need not narrow and limit teaching and learning; broad
national agreement about the 5–16 curriculum and the objectives of its
various parts if applied to all pupils would improve the individual
curricular programmes of many thousands of pupils; and well-founded
arrangements for school self-evaluation and teacher appraisal would
not only improve the delivery of education within individual schools,
but would also lead to more effective professional and career
development of individual teachers which, in turn, should lead to
genuine improvements in the performance of pupils of all abilities
across the 5–16 age range. That improvement, in the end, is what all
the inter-related parts of the school education service exist to bring
about.

Assessment Techniques and Approaches

2.1 Public Examinations

Paper by the Department of Education and Science

The Cockcroft Report[1] records the following remark drawn to the attention of the Committee in the course of its inquiry: 'No one has ever grown taller as a result of being measured' (page 123). But this remark has only limited application to the measurement of performance by secondary school examinations. Leaving to one side the great demand from certain sections of society, notably parents, further and higher education bodies and employers, to know how 'tall' pupils are, it is widely recognised that, in its broader sense, assessment by examinations can have two positive purposes — diagnosis and recording — the one analysing pupils' performance and identifying weaknesses in order to remedy them, the other recognising achievements attained. Both purposes can help motivate pupils to achieve more and attain a higher level of performance. With the correct measuring instrument pupils can be encouraged, in performance terms, to grow taller. The question is how the public examinations system can be made more effective as a measuring instrument; this paper describes proposed changes in the system that should lead to its better fulfilling the two purposes outlined above.

The examination and assessment of pupils can also contribute to the assessment of their schools and teachers, with the same purposes — diagnosis and recording. Interpreted with care, these measurements of pupils can encourage schools and teachers alike to grow taller.

Background

Better Schools set out the following specific objectives with regard to examinations taken at school:

    i. to raise standards across the whole ability range;
    ii. to support improvements in the curriculum and in the way in which it is taught;
    iii. to provide clear aims for teachers and pupils, to the benefit of both and of higher education and employers;
    iv. to record proven achievement;

---

[1] DES. *Mathematics Counts*. Report of the Committee of Inquiry into the Teaching of Mathematics in Schools, under the Chairmanship of Dr W H (now Sir Wilfred) Cockcroft. HMSO, 1982.

    v. to promote the measurement of achievement based on what candidates know, understand and can do;

    vi. to broaden the studies of pupils in the 4th and 5th secondary years and of 6th form students.

The intention is, therefore, to improve examinations by designing them to support, rather than dominate, curricular objectives, and through these means to raise standards. *Better Schools* envisaged the securing of national agreement about curricular objectives and the use of appropriately designed examinations to measure pupils' performance against assessment objectives set in the light of those curricular objectives. This assessment would serve the same purposes mentioned earlier, namely diagnosis and recording: examinations would play an important part in securing the effective delivery within schools of the nationally agreed curricular objectives and would record the positive achievements of pupils.

The General Certificate of Secondary Education (GCSE)

The reforms of the 16-plus examination system are designed to set in place at the end of the compulsory period of schooling an examination system that would meet the six objectives outlined above.

Agreed assessment objectives

i.   The national criteria for the GCSE represent agreement among those concerned on the frameworks within which syllabuses will be drawn up for particular subjects. As the Secretaries of State for Education and Science and for Wales said in their foreword to *The National Criteria*[1]: 'For the first time, the partners in the education service have pooled their wisdom and experience in order to produce nationally-agreed statements on course objectives, content and assessment methods for all the subject areas most commonly examined in the final years of compulsory schooling'. The national criteria for individual subjects were drawn up in the light of best practice and developments within those subjects and should result in improved examination syllabuses and examination courses. They specify objectives both for the examination courses and for assessment. For the first time there is an agreed description of skills, abilities and competencies which pupils will need to foster and demonstrate as a result of two-year public examination courses. The criteria are not, of course, meant to constitute a straitjacket. As the debate on curricular objectives continues, they may require revision; the Secondary Examinations Council (SEC) has the responsibility of reviewing them periodically and suggesting changes where required.

---

[1] GCSE: *The National Criteria*. HMSO, 1985.

Agreed course content

ii.   The national criteria, by laying down guidelines within which
syllabuses must be drawn up, should help to reduce the number of
separate syllabuses, and subject titles, currently presented for 16-plus
examinations. In addition, the separate examination boards, by
working together within five GCSE Examining Groups, will help
further to reduce the plethora of near-identical syllabuses and ensure
that teachers, users of certificates and others concerned can have
greater confidence that an examination course title represents an
agreed delineation and description of the course content.

Measurement of a wider range of positive achievements

iii.   The requirement for differentiated papers, or differentiated
questions within common papers, in all GCSE subjects should enable
all pupils to be awarded grades on a more positive performance than
hitherto. It is intended that pupils will be assessed on the basis of good
performance on questions of varying difficulty, so that able pupils are
tested to their full ability and less able pupils no longer, as now often
happens, merely pick up a few marks from poor performances on
questions which are too difficult for them. By pupils being required,
particularly for the achievement of the lower grades, to give a wider
and more positive demonstration of their abilities than under the
current system a more reliable measure of attainment will be possible.

iv.   The national criteria also provide for GCSE examinations in
almost all subjects to include a significant element of course work, as
well as timed written examinations. The setting and assessment of
coursework can help teaching and learning processes by measuring —
and thus encouraging the development of — important skills not easily
tested by timed, written examinations alone. Practical and oral skills
are amongst those to be emphasised.

More objective grading

v.   In existing 16-plus examinations the award of grades to individual
candidates is largely norm-referenced — heavily influenced by the
relative overall performance of all candidates. The GCSE, when first
introduced, will also be essentially norm-referenced, though the
changes and developments outlined above (and, in particular, in
paragraph iii, above) should go a long way to reducing the harmful
effects of such a system, particularly for pupils of lower abilities. The
intention however is to move as quickly as practicable to a new and
more objective system of 'criteria-related' grading in which the grades
awarded will be based more closely on recognised standards and
defined levels of attainment, without reference to the performance of
other candidates.

vi.   This is an ambitious and important development, still in its
infancy. The SEC has recently, as a first step, published for

consultation the grade criteria proposals for 10 subjects. Working from the national criteria, they have attempted to define the aspects of each subject in which pupils' attainment will be assessed, and to define the level of attainment expected of candidates in each of those aspects for the award of particular grades. Much work remains to be done, but the prizes are high. Grade criteria are more than just an attempt to make the grade awarded a better and more objective reflection of candidates' abilities, and thus more helpful to employers and other users of certificates; they ought also, by specifying what needs to be achieved for the award of particular grades, to set clear goals for pupils to aim at and thus help to motivate them to attain more.

Post-16 examinations in schools

Traditionally, most pupils who have remained at school post-16 have done so in order to take A-levels — an examination which has its roots in universities' requirements for properly grounded candidates from amongst whom they can select their degree entrants. Since A-levels are designed for a limited ability range, and there are no plans for systematically basing their award on criteria-related grades, they are likely to be of limited value in the assessment of a school's performance, although carefully interpreted A-level results can throw light on how well a school develops the potential of its ablest pupils.§

The Government stated its commitment in *Better Schools* to the retention of A-levels, noting not only their role in providing a foundation, and selecting entrants, for degree courses, but also the standards of excellence which they set. Since then, it has been announced that there are to be certain changes to the A-level grading system which, *inter alia*, will introduce an explicit but limited element of criterion-referencing into the existing, largely norm-referenced system. This development, taken with the work done by the GCE boards in relation to common cores for the most popular A-level subjects, follows to some extent the trend of the developments in the 16-plus examination system outlined above (paragraphs ii. and iii., p41), but at the present time there are no plans to introduce agreed assessment objectives for A-levels to parallel the GCSE national criteria; the A-level examination continues to determine curricular objectives for this period of study.

The Government's objective (vi., page 40) that examinations should broaden the study of senior pupils included a specific reference to sixth form students. The new sixth form examination — the Advanced Supplementary (AS) level — which is to be introduced in autumn 1987 has been designed to encourage A-level students to broaden their examined studies. This additional measure of performance, taken with A-level performance, will provide a somewhat fuller assessment of each pupil and could contribute to the overall evaluation of a school's sixth form work — though with the proviso in paragraph § above.

The nature of sixth forms has changed, however, over the last two decades. Provision has increasingly been made for those who are neither taking A-level courses nor re-taking O-levels. To meet the needs of these 'new' sixth formers, a range of new courses have been offered by a variety of examining and validating bodies; from autumn 1985 much of this provision has been subsumed within the Certificate of Pre-Vocational Education (CPVE). In the CPVE, assessment is not based upon timed, written examinations; instead, as with its predecessors, there will mainly be continuous assessment of candidates by their schools, with those schools being subject to validation and moderation by the examining and validating bodies. This process provides regular feedback for teachers and pupils, and allows the assessment to serve the purpose of diagnosis as well as recording, with encouraging effects on motivation and performance.

Public examinations — contribution to the appraisal and evaluation of performance

Pupils' performance

The examination reforms outlined above should lead to a fuller and fairer assessment of pupils' performance, in particular at age 16 where the GCSE's increased emphasis on coursework assessment should provide opportunities for pupils to learn more about their strengths and weaknesses; for achievements to be properly reinforced; and for consequential improvements in motivation and performance.

The Secretary of State for Education and Science has set as a national objective 'to raise pupil performance at all levels of ability so as to bring 80–90 per cent of all 16 year-old pupils at least to the level of attainment now expected and achieved by pupils of average ability in individual subjects'. The development of grade criteria for the GCSE, defining levels of attainment, will be a necessary pre-requisite for monitoring whether this objective is being met at national, LEA and/or school levels.

Schools' and teachers' performance

The use of public examination results as an output measurement in the appraisal and evaluation of schools and/or teachers is fraught with such obvious difficulties that it can be tempting for those professionally concerned to eschew their use completely. Yet parents and other outside interest groups will draw conclusions — often unwarranted — from schools' examination results, and schools and teachers will themselves find that methods of appraisal and evaluation that place too little weight on the examination results achieved by pupils will be inadequate. GCSE examination results, interpreted with care, ought in the future to provide some insight into pupils' standards of learning during the compulsory, secondary phase of schooling and, therefore, contribute to the appraisal and evaluation of schools and teachers. However, much that is of value in what schools and teachers develop in pupils will, as now, not be amenable to measurement through examinations.

In any such interpretation of examination results, due allowance would have to be made for the many variables affecting pupils' performance. The DES *Statistical Bulletin 13/84*[1] identified three main sets of variables — socio-economic (eg. socio-economic group of the head of household, rate of unemployment); resource (eg. expenditure per pupil); and school-based (eg. school size, teacher turnover, parent: teacher ratio [PTR]) — and indicated the correlation between examination results and each and all of these background variables, commenting on their statistical significance. All the findings were at the level of the LEA. The bulletin described a number of difficulties regarding the interpretation of the statistical results, but nevertheless offered an analysis of examination results at local authority level which took account of the variables identified and yet revealed differences remaining and unaccounted for. The DES *Pilot Study of School Examination Performance and Associated Factors*[2] reports the results of a parallel study, employing similar analytical techniques, but at the level of the individual school. This concluded that the relationship between socio-economic background factors and examination results revealed at the LEA level also appears to operate at the level of the individual school; but acknowledged that the problem of taking proper account of socio-economic factors at school level had not been fully solved.

The Secretary of State has judged that further work of this kind would most profitably be done, if it proves feasible, at the level of the school, and has invited proposals for such work which the Department might support. A number of such proposals are under consideration.

---

[1] *School Standards and Spending: Statistical Analysis: A further appreciation* (Statistical Bulletin 13/84). DES, 1984.

[2] Darlington J K and Cullen B (1984). *Pilot Study of School Examination Performance and Associated Factors* (Government Economic Service Working Paper No. 75). DES 1984.

Assessment Techniques and Approaches

2.2 Records of Achievement

Paper by the Department of Education and Science

The Government has set the policy objective (*Better Schools*, paragraph 116) of 'establishing by the end of the decade arrangements under which all pupils [in England and Wales] leaving school will be provided with a record of achievement'. This record would contain details not only of successes in public examinations but also of other educational attainments and of personal qualities: it would be as full a record as possible of the positive achievements of school leavers.

Background

The potential value of such records has been recognised for many years. The Newsom Report, *Half our Future*[1], commented that 'boys and girls who stay at school until they are 16 may reasonably look for some record of achievement when they leave'. Public examination results have offered, and will continue to offer, only a partial record for a proportion of pupils — though these results will be a fuller and fairer measure of outcome for an increasing number of pupils once the GCSE has been introduced. What has been identified — by those in schools and outside — as necessary in addition is a record for all pupils of their knowledge and skills in other areas of the curriculum, and of experiences and achievements which reflect personal and social qualities not tested by examinations.

A number of LEAs and schools have developed and already make use of such records; profiles also play an important part in certain courses (in particular those offered under the Technical and Vocational Education Initiative (TVEI) and those validated by further education examining bodies) now being taken by pupils in schools. Those involved in developing records have seen these as providing a better and fuller assessment of pupils with beneficial effects on pupil motivation. But the titles, purposes, format and content of the various profiles and records developed differ considerably and have as yet little national recognition.

The Government responded to this accelerating but fragmented development of pupil records by publishing a draft policy statement on records of achievement in November 1983, finalising this in July 1984

---

[1] HMSO 1963 (reprinted 1966).

in the light of the very large number of welcoming and constructive responses to the draft that were received[1]. The Government announced that a number of pilot schemes would be funded in order to gain more experience, and with a view to establishing the greatest possible degree of agreement on the main issues. A national steering committee would take responsibility for the monitoring and evaluation of these schemes and report to the Secretaries of State for Education and Science and for Wales in the autumn of 1988, offering draft guidelines for the proposed national introduction of records of achievement for all pupils in secondary schools by the end of the decade.

Purposes of records of achievement

There is widespread agreement on the following purposes, set out in paragraph 11 of the Government's policy statement on records of achievement, though not all would give each purpose the same emphasis:

'i. *Recognition of achievement.* Records and recording systems should recognise, acknowledge and give credit for what pupils have achieved and experienced, not just in terms of public examinations but in other ways as well. They should do justice to pupils' own efforts and to the efforts of teachers, parents, ratepayers and taxpayers to give them a good education.

ii. *Motivation and personal development.* Records and recording systems should contribute to pupils' personal development and progress by improving their motivation, providing encouragement and increasing their awareness of strengths, weaknesses and opportunities.

iii. *Curriculum and organisation.* The recording process should help schools to identify the all-round potential of their pupils and to consider how well their curriculum, teaching and organisation enable pupils to develop the general, practical and social skills which are to be recorded.

iv. *A document of record.* Young people leaving school or college should take with them a short, summary document of record which is recognised and valued by employers and institutions of further and higher education. This should provide a more rounded picture of candidates for jobs or courses than can be provided by a list of examination results, thus helping potential users to decide how candidates could best be

---

[1] *Records of Achievement at 16: A Statement of Policy.* DES, 1984. See also *Records of Achievement at 16. Some examples of current practice.* HMSO, 1985. (Originally issued by DES, 1983).

employed, or for which jobs, training schemes or courses they are likely to be suitable.'

Issues still to be resolved

The nine pilot schemes in England and Wales, financed under the arrangements for Education Support Grants[1], have been chosen to illustrate a variety of different approaches to those issues already identified as still to be resolved: namely, the relative importance of the purposes given in the preceding paragraph; the content and form of records; the recording processes (including the techniques to be used for assessing personal qualities); and national currency and accreditation. Other issues are already emerging, and more may well arise during the piloting. One issue, which can be little more than noted at this stage, is the developing relationship between records of achievement and other forms of certification and the influence that each will have on the other.

The guidelines to be produced by the national steering committee are intended to provide a clear framework for national policy whilst leaving scope for local variations. If records of achievement are to have national currency with employers and further and higher education, they will almost certainly require a common format and some defined common characteristics. They will probably need also to be subject to an agreed and respected form of validation or accreditation. However it is likely to be unnecessary and undesirable for the guidelines to be too detailed or prescriptive.

The introduction of records of achievement will highlight certain issues that schools already have to address: the need for simple and effective internal recording systems and reporting arrangements; and the transfer of data between schools, whether for all pupils as they move from primary to secondary schools and perhaps in addition make a further move at 16, or for individual pupils as they move in or out of schools at any point in time. The Government's policy statement envisaged that, for the purposes of records of achievement, pupils' internal records would be developed throughout the secondary phase and would begin with a summary of achievements by the end of the primary phase; how that summary is to be produced, and what it is to contain, is still for consideration. Since records of achievement are to be for the secondary school leaver, whether at 16, 17 or 18, there is the further issue of how the record of a 17 or 18 year-old should compare with that of a 16 year-old and the possibility (mentioned earlier) of problems of continuity between 11–16 schools and sixth form colleges.

---

[1] See also *Education Support Grants*. DES Circular 5/85. (Explains the Education Support Grants Regulations 1984, as amended 1985.)

Records of achievement — contribution to performance appraisal and evaluation

Pupils' performance

Previous development work on records has demonstrated clear benefits to pupils from the internal, formative processes of reporting, recording and discussion. These internal processes, in providing opportunities for pupils to learn more about, and reflect more on, their own needs and to have their achievements positively reinforced, have been shown to lead to improvements in pupils' motivation and performance.

It is intended that the final, summative record, with its emphasis on the 'whole pupil', should provide a fuller measure of pupils' performance than would otherwise be available through published examination results. Provided that these records, when introduced, command the confidence of parents, employers, careers officers and institutions of further and higher education, they will enable pupils to be selected for jobs or courses with the help of a more rounded picture of their abilities — and therefore more appropriately in some instances.

Schools' and teachers' performance

The drawing-up of the internal, formative records, rooted in two-way discussions between teacher and pupil, should provide insights for teachers into the changes that may be necessary not only in pupils' individual programmes but, more importantly, in the school's curriculum and in its teaching and organisation (cf purpose iii., page 46) and thus aid teachers' and schools' self evaluation.

There may be possibilities for those professionally concerned within the school and LEA to use the final, summative records as part of their evaluation of what pupils in their schools and/or authorities have achieved in the non-examined areas of the curriculum and also in cross-curricular and extra-curricular school activities. The Government's policy statement envisages the ownership of the final, summative record lying firmly with the pupil, with schools retaining master copies in order to meet reasonable requests from pupils for duplicates but requiring pupils' permission before supplying copies to anyone else. Any use of these records for evaluative purposes should have regard to the need to secure proper protection of the information in them.

Implications for LEAs and central government

If the successful introduction of records of achievement and the contribution to the evaluation and appraisal of performance outlined above are to be secured, there are implications for LEAs and central government in respect of the proper support for teachers through initial and in service training. Teachers will need help in acquiring:

i. appropriate assessment skills (in particular, the techniques for assessing personal qualities and for constructive discussions with pupils);

ii. a better understanding of the close inter-relation between assessment, the curriculum and the teaching process; and

iii. any additional knowledge and skills that may be needed to implement the curricular and organisation changes — and the changes in teaching methods — that are revealed as necessary during the compilation of records of achievement.

There are also implications for schools' staffing and organisation if teachers are to have adequate time to undertake the production, with pupils, of records of achievement; to learn from that process; and to introduce any curricular and teaching changes that may be needed. The recently published report of the joint DES/local authority working group on schoolteacher numbers and deployment in the longer term[1] makes explicit allowance for records of achievement in its assessment of the additional teacher time which might be associated with the implementation of Government policies for the schools. That report and its conclusions are now under consideration by Ministers and elected members.

---

[1] *Report of the Working Group on Schoolteacher Numbers and Deployment in the Longer Term.* DES, 1984.

Assessment Techniques and Approaches

2.3 Testing — Fitness for Purpose

Paper by Her Majesty's Inspectorate

Suspicion of testing has a long history. Examinations to select entrants into the Imperial Civil Service were established in China by the seventh century, becoming increasingly elaborate and, according to their critics, increasingly inimical to the cause of education. Would-be reformers protested at their rigidity and their demands for stylised and anachronistic responses from candidates. Success, it was claimed, could be gained only by a style of teaching which stultified thinking and did little to promote genuine learning. 'Scholar' came to acquire a peculiar usage equating to 'uselessness'.

Similar anxieties about the undesirable impact of testing remain: fuelled perhaps by memories of some of the more exaggerated claims made in support of selection tests at 11-plus. They are frequently expressed as fears about the evils of competition and the dangers of reinforcing failure, or about the incapacity of tests accurately to predict future performance. Testing is held to be self-fulfilling not only with regard to how teachers view their pupils but also in the sense that it reduces curriculum objectives to those that are susceptible to tests. Its perceived inadequacies are seen as a brake on curriculum development.

Many of these concerns have some force. But often they rest upon a view of testing which takes a particular model as its paradigm. It is a model which is very close to the form taken by some public examinations and standardised tests. Its characteristic features are that it is formal, norm-referenced, relies heavily upon information recall and serves a limited number of purposes usually concerned with institutional policies of selection and placement. Testing is seen as picking out only those procedures which take place in special sessions under more or less controlled conditions set apart from day-to-day activities. Yet despite the many misgivings it provokes, this is still the model often employed, more especially in secondary schools.

Confronted with this paradox much recent discussion and activity has attempted to expand the frame of reference by highlighting approaches to testing which are less obtrusive and of wider value. In part this has drawn attention to the growing range of techniques and vehicles, oral and practical as well as written, which are available. In conducting its surveys the Assessment of Performance Unit (APU) has described frameworks for assessment and how to use them, and has initiated many new techniques of testing. The merits of structured observation of pupils' activities in the classroom — of group discussion for example — are gradually being recognised and implemented. Much of the concern, however, has been directed towards a reconsideration of the purposes for which testing is undertaken and, as a necessary corollary, the bases on which comparisons of performance are made. The development of GCSE examinations, for example, has been one part of a movement away from comparisons between individuals and towards comparisons made against external criteria; from norm-referencing to criterion-referencing.

Set alongside testing's typical purpose of selection, therefore, have been its more dynamic uses in diagnosing individual strengths and weaknesses, identifying potential aptitudes and abilities and evaluating the effectiveness of teaching methods and curricular provision. Although variously expressed, recent analyses of the purposes of testing maintain in common the contention that the function of assessment is to enhance pupils' performance, not merely to furnish information by which that performance can be recorded and reported.

The HMI discussion document on *The Curriculum from 5 to 16*[1], for example, while it recognises the traditional role of assessment in guiding pupils into appropriate courses and groups, stresses that 'assessment is inseparable from the teaching process since its prime purpose is to improve pupils' performance'. Both here and in the White Paper, *Better Schools,* it is the central and positive function assessment must necessarily have in the whole teaching and learning process which is emphasised: its role in enabling teachers and schools to appraise their teaching objectives and approaches, and as an integral part of the curriculum.

Fitness for purpose

Crucial to the enterprise of translating these broad functions into effective practice is the criterion of fitness for purpose. The minimal conditions which this criterion requires are that:

  i. the particular purpose for which testing is undertaken must be unambiguous and matched to appropriate procedures;

  ii. testing procedures should be used which minimise potentially damaging side-effects; and

  iii. they must be consistent with the aims and objectives embodied in the curriculum and the teaching strategies employed.

These conditions are not easily satisfied.

---

[1] *The Curriculum from 5 to 16* (Curriculum Matters No. 2). HMSO, 1985.

In practice the distinction between purposes can become blurred. Diagnosis and evaluation, for example, may readily slip into selection and grading. Yet the procedures required are essentially different. For selection the prime requirement is successful discrimination. This success depends upon testing techniques which are capable of eliciting both correct and incorrect responses, enabling comparisons to be made between pupils. Thus multiple choice items which pre-testing shows not to have adequate indices of discrimination, which fail to spread out the scores of those attempting them, are automatically rejected. But this is not relevant to testing where the purpose is diagnosis. This needs to provide information about where pupils have gone wrong and where they have been successful, not an indication of their comparative achievements. Were all to succeed it would be a source of satisfaction rather than embarrassment. Similarly, standardised tests which report results in terms of predetermined norms can yield valuable information where the purpose is to screen groups of pupils. The more precisely focused the purpose becomes, upon individual guidance or particular classroom practice, the greater the degree of caution which has to be exercised in utilising their results.

There are additional factors to weigh in determining fitness. Assessment processes are distinguished not solely, perhaps not even primarily, by the techniques they employ. They often depend crucially upon matters of emphasis and timing; that is, upon what precisely is being assessed and when. Currently, for example, one of the weakest areas of assessment is of the higher order skills — skills of interpretation, analysis and evaluation — where a major problem is that assessment items which aim to test such skills cannot with confidence be classified as doing so uniquely. The classification varies from pupil to pupil. For example, an item which explores what is an unfamiliar situation for one pupil may, as a result of wider reading or greater experience, be totally familiar to another. What is posed as a problem to be resolved may, in practice, be answered on the basis of information recall. This is simply to instance one way in which a gap between assessment objectives and procedures may emerge — albeit, perhaps, unwittingly.

When assessment takes place, whether terminally, periodically or continuously, has clear implications for what is assessed and for pupils' response to it. Timing is obviously significant in any decision on whether the emphasis is to be upon process or product. Equally, as staged assessment recognises, it may crucially affect pupils' motivation and hence their performance.

These types of distinctions might be summarised under the two broad categories of formative and summative assessment, which, in effect, pull considerations of purpose, emphasis and timing together. Neither category retains exclusive hold on particular forms of assessment. Rather they pick out the intentions of the assessor and the interpretations put upon the information acquired. The one focuses upon facilitating improvements in performance, the other upon reporting performance. Thus, they offer a helpful way into the complexities of match by requiring of the teacher an initial establishment of assessment priorities.

Partly as an accompaniment to the process of identifying the wider purposes of assessment, and partly also in response to the kind of undesirable side-effects noted earlier, there have been growing reservations about norm-referencing and an increasing emphasis given to criterion referencing. Certainly there can be seen in criterion-referenced procedures a fruitful reconsideration of the central issues of decision-making about assessment. There is a potential danger, however, in some of the present discussion in that it tends to polarise the distinction — both in terms of their respective procedures and of their respective virtues and vices. In neither sense, perhaps, are they discrete. When almost any test example is looked at in detail norms may be found influencing criteria or, though more rarely, vice versa. It seems more useful, therefore, to ask of a test not whether the result is analysed with respect to norms or criteria, but how the two interact: what part each plays in the setting up, marking and interpretation of results. It is not clear how far ipsative referencing, which judges pupils against their own previous performance, offers a further alternative to norm-referencing. Arguably it represents a more informal, if shifting, form of criterion-referencing. Its main strength may be the requirement it places upon the teacher to have the particular pupil firmly in sight when determining assessment criteria.

The third of the necessary conditions which it was suggested fitness for purpose must meet (iii, page 51) requires an inter-relationship between teaching and testing practices which can be justified by curriculum objectives. This is not achieved where the means employed to test a skill do not match the way in which the skill is taught; where for example, recognition of words in isolation is the procedure employed for test reading ability. Nor is it achieved if teachers exclude curricular objectives on the grounds that they do not appear in the particular public examination for which their pupils are entered.

Assessment which satisfies the conditions picked out by fitness for purpose imposes heavy demands. It requires of the teacher not merely an understanding of the range of techniques — the ability to construct valid multiple-choice or objective items, for example, or to structure questions appropriately — but a perceptive awareness of their strengths and limitations. Questions which strictly circumscribe possible responses may produce highly reliable results, but at the cost of limiting pupils' flair and creativity. Determining fitness for purpose depends upon insights into what makes a question difficult. Is it the way in which the task is presented or the nature of the material the question contains, rather than ignorance, which is preventing the pupil from demonstrating the required skill or conceptual understanding? Is the ability to form a written response necessarily the only reliable indicator of performance? These and other considerations are insistently and continually raised for the teacher concerned with assessment.

Fitness for purpose is centrally concerned with test validity. It has been the focus here because it is in terms of its validity that much of what currently takes place under assessment is open to question. However valid, assessment cannot of itself improve performance or raise standards — the crucial issue is reaction to the outcome of assessment — but any reaction to invalid procedures is of little worth.

Assessment Techniques and Approaches

2.4 The Work of the Assessment of Performance Unit

Paper by the Department of Education and Science

The APU was established in 1975:

> 'to promote the development of methods of assessing and monitoring the achievement of children at school, and to seek to identify the incidence of under-achievement.'

The Unit was to provide, for the first time, information about the performance of all pupils, not just those taking public examinations. It was to provide a measure of pupil performance which would inform public debate and monitor any changes in performance which might occur over time.

Since then the following national surveys of pupil performance have been undertaken on the basis of samples:

At age 11 and 15 in:
   Mathematics, annually 1978–82
   English language, annually 1979–83

At age 11, 13 and 15 in:
   Science, annually 1980–84

At age 13 in:
   Foreign languages: French 1983, 1984 and 1985;
                      German and Spanish in 1983.

The Unit has also made a contribution to the debate about curricular issues by suggesting frameworks for assessment in other areas: physical development, aesthetic development, personal and social development, and design and technology. It is now starting to develop test items in this last field for a survey in 1988.

In November 1982 the Secretary of State for Education and Science announced that the initial phase of annual monitoring in the areas of mathematics, English and science would be followed by a programme of periodic monitoring, at intervals of five years in each case. The period between the surveys is to be used to undertake further analyses of the data already accumulated to make some in-depth probes and to disseminate the findings. The next survey in mathematics will be in 1987, in English in 1988 and in science in 1989.

As information has become available from the Unit's national surveys it has become clear that they are providing a detailed picture of pupil performance of a kind which has not hitherto been available and which it would have been difficult to envisage in 1975. They reveal a complex pattern of performance. For example, the mathematics surveys show that 50 per cent of 11 year-olds are able to add correctly 5.07 and 1.3. They also show that of the 20 per cent who did least well in APU's mathematical tests overall there was still a group (9 per cent in all) which was able to arrive at the correct answer. Seventy-eight common errors in mathematics have been listed. Such analysis goes beyond the identification of tasks which pupils find difficult, and begins to explore the nature of the difficulty.

The APU findings also point to common errors pupils make (in language, for example, by failing to distinguish between what is written and what is hinted at, or what is in their memory and has come from other sources). The Unit now has extensive evidence to indicate that many pupils have a fragile grasp of ideas and processes which by common consent were believed to be easy. Procedural skills (such as making notes whilst the teacher speaks, or measuring and estimating) have been assumed to be easy to master, and the APU findings have demonstrated that many pupils have not mastered them. In other areas pupils have done better than expected; for example in attempting practical investigations and in picking out the general sense from extended texts in a foreign language.

The work of the APU can now be seen to have uncovered specific and major blockages to learning, some of which are crucial because their removal could allow pupils to move towards significantly higher achievement over a relatively broad front. It is apparent from APU tests that many pupils cannot, for example, measure accurately. If that blockage could be removed, pupils would be better placed to achieve more in later work in science and technology. Many pupils have also been shown to have a poor grasp of place value: if this could be remedied, pupils would have a better chance to develop computational and measuring skills. Moreover, pupils' strengths have been identified and these can be built upon.

The APU has used a broad framework of assessment in its surveys — broad enough to reflect adequately what teachers are trying to teach. Individual pupils are, however, asked to attempt only a small part of the total number of test items used in each survey. The tests administered to individual pupils last no more than an hour in the case of primary-age pupils, or no more than a double period in the case of secondary pupils. The results are aggregated to provide a national picture of pupil performance. The APU's tests and assessment procedures, developed for national monitoring, are not directly applicable to the testing of individual children. Further information on individual pupils' performance on different types of questions may emerge from deeper analysis of the data. The survey findings have indicated many profitable lines of research which could improve opportunities for pupils. Many of these might be more appropriately undertaken by other agencies. There is a good model in science where work has been commissioned outside APU to turn APU findings into new ways of working in schools (*Children's learning in science* project — Leeds University).

It is not the task of the APU to suggest what action in terms of the curriculum or approaches to teaching may be appropriate in the light of its findings. The Unit has, however, taken steps through changes in the style and format of its publications, notably in the new series of short reports aimed specifically at the classroom teacher, to bring its findings to the attention of as wide an audience as possible. DES has commissioned and is publishing independent appraisals of the implications of APU work in mathematics, English language and science[1].

Extracting the potential value for schools

There are four readily usable assets:

i. In designing test instruments APU has unpacked the curriculum making clear what are the important things. These instruments enable assessment of particular aspects of performance to be made and moreover they often do so in the context of a task which is interesting and purposeful for pupils. The testing of isolated fragments of knowledge and skills has been largely avoided. In looking at APU test materials teachers might ask:

> 'What facet is this testing? Have my pupils been taught in such a way that they could respond well?'

Since APU tests are broad its test items can provide a curriculum checklist, with the proviso that there are some things which remain outside testing.

APU assessment has looked at PROCESSES AND PROCEDURES of learning in addition to concepts. This has made clear what pupils might learn in areas such as observation, evaluation of data, speaking and listening, problem solving. There are booklets for teachers, and videos and in-service workshop materials are available. Many of the test items themselves are published for teachers to consider.

ii. About one thousand teachers have been trained to make assessments by APU. They report BENEFICIAL EFFECTS FOR THEIR OWN TEACHING. They are a useful fieldforce to help others to consider the value of the APU workshop materials.

---

[1] An *APU list of publications* is available, free, from Room 4/77A, DES, Elizabeth House, York Road, London SE1 7PH. (See also Bibliography.)

iii. The detailed description of pupils' responses into levels of performance with many errors exposed and analysed is providing A LEARNING MAP which should inform teaching. This is a challenge to some parts of teachers' teaching schemes.

iv. In the realm of ideas APU evidence supports a view that learning is about changing the schema which pupils hold in their minds as they interpret the meaning of events. Pupils' mental schema are very different from those, for example, of the adult scientist and mathematician. Pupils need learning opportunities which support them in generating new mental models. The LEARNER IS AN ACTIVE CONSTRUCTOR of understanding.

APU assessment frameworks, instruments, ways of testing and descriptions of pupils' responses provide illuminating insight into curriculum, teaching and assessing. APU materials can enable teachers to develop professional judgement in their capacity to assess and to place less reliance on mechanical testing.

Further progress is possible, if:

i. Teachers can find TIME TO GAIN EXPERIENCE with individual pupils and with other teachers in trying out some of the APU methods.

ii. Action research can convert APU items into diagnostic tests of a robust nature for use in school. The APU test items specifically designed for surveys are too delicate and time-consuming for direct use by schools for diagnostic or summative assessment.

iii. Research involving teachers can develop classroom teaching strategies to prevent pupils making common errors.

Assessment Techniques and Approaches

2.5 Inspection

Paper by Her Majesty's Inspectorate

The term 'Inspection' is usually associated with an external appraisal of an organisation or institution, either in whole or in part, carried out by an individual or group who, having regard for certain criteria, provide expertise, objectivity and a breadth of view. The nature, range and purposes of inspections vary and may be concerned with one or more dimensions of the institution. For example, an inspection may concentrate on the systems in a school, such as its curriculum or staffing; or on processes, such as the teaching taking place in classrooms or the interaction between pupils and between pupils and teachers about the school generally; or on outputs, such as the attainment levels of the children. An inspection could be concerned with all of these dimensions and the method of inspection used would vary accordingly.

Much of the inspection of schools is undertaken by Her Majesty's Inspectorate (HMI) to whose practices the ensuing paragraphs mainly refer, and whose role and work are explored more fully in the Annex to this paper (page 65). But a key element in the monitoring of the educational system is the work of advisers and inspectors employed by LEAs. They provide assessments of the quality of education in institutions, act as agents for change, give direct support to individual teachers, and are involved in the development and implementation of plans derived from local and national initiatives. Their role, focused as it is on the local situation, complements that of HMI, who are concerned with standards nationally and whose reports, such as those on the findings of major surveys undertaken in recent years in primary, secondary, first and middle schools, provide an assessment of the quality of aspects of education across the country.

Types of inspection

HM Inspectorate's central task is to report on the standards of learning achieved. To this end there is no single inspection procedure which covers all situations and the purpose of a particular exercise affects its design. Moreover, such designs are usually refined on the evidence of pilot trials and in the light of experience.

Many visits are made by individual inspectors or by teams working to an agreed brief; these lead to records which are kept in the

Inspectorate's working files on each school, or to short reports for the information of those members of HMI with a special interest in the field being looked at.

Inspections leading to a report to the Secretary of State* tend to be longer and to involve more personnel. A full inspection of a single institution may involve a team of inspectors spending a week or so in a school. Usually one member of the team acts as co-ordinator, or reporting inspector (RI), and a panel is assembled whose joint interests and expertise match the objectives of the inspection. The aim is to assemble the smallest team capable of providing the specialist cover required and staying long enough in the institution to inspect it thoroughly. In general, the full inspection of a primary school will require two to four inspectors each spending three to four days in the school, although these arrangements are modified in the light of the size of the school and the presence of particular elements, such as a special education unit. Teams for the inspections of secondary schools would be considerably larger, amounting perhaps for an 11–18 school with 1,000 pupils to up to 12 full-time and three or four or more part-time inspectors over the course of a week.

The inspections of single institutions in England may also be carried out under the Inspectorate's programme of short inspections for primary and secondary schools, introduced in 1982. Here the intention is that a representative sample — of around 100 primary and 50 secondary schools chosen by computer according to criteria such as size, age-range, status and location — is inspected annually, and these inspections provide much of the information used by HMI to write evaluative summaries. Full inspections of primary schools are carried out under this programme, but the short inspections of secondary schools, although of a week's duration, do not look at all aspects of a school and the reports concentrate on the teaching and learning, the curriculum and the school as a community.

In recent years, too, a programme for the review of the educational provision of a single LEA has been developed and reports are written on some two or three LEAs each year. The main inspection period for these exercises may span a year or more and include visits which range widely from full inspections to those made for one day to single institutions by subject or phase specialists. In this way a representative sample of the provision in institutions of varying types within an authority is sought to provide a basis for judgements.

As part of its national sampling HM Inspectorate also undertakes a number of surveys aimed at raising relevant questions and wherever possible coming to conclusions on the evidence of what has been seen.

---

* ie. the Secretary of State for Education and Science, or in Wales, the Secretary of State for Wales. The paper is based on procedures current in England, though, apart from some differences of detail, it is equally valid for Wales.

In setting up such surveys HMI has the guidance and assistance of the Statistical Information Unit (SIU), especially in the selection of appropriate samples. These surveys may take several years to complete and, as in the case of the current survey of teacher training institutions, may involve HMI in making more than one visit to the same place and incorporate some full inspections.

Criteria

HMI do not impose externally decided criteria but develop these from their observations of best practice and seek to make them known through reports and publications. In reaching judgements regard is paid to criteria whose nature and range will vary with the type of inspection being undertaken. The criteria will also be related to what are judged by the inspectors to be reasonable points of reference or norms, and such norms are unlikely to change from year to year, or from school to school. For example, satisfactory teaching, wherever it takes place, will have certain consistent indicators such as evidence that lessons are being planned and prepared in relation to a scheme of work, that the teaching methods and resources used are varied and matched to the abilities of the pupils, that there is evidence of appropriate pacing and the good use of time, and that the pupils' work, in whatever form it is presented, is supportively and constructively assessed.

In coming to judgements on the work in classrooms, inspectors need to consider the quality of both the teaching and the learning. HMI do not report on individual teachers but evaluate the teaching. They have regard for criteria such as: whether the teacher's expectations of the pupils are appropriate; whether there is progression in the work; whether the teaching stimulates interest, curiosity, enthusiasm, initiative and a responsibility on the part of the pupil for organising studies, in addition to a mastery of the content of the material being taught; whether the teaching methods, books and materials are suited to the age, aptitude, and ability of the pupil; and whether the teaching is influenced by the condition and suitability of the accommodation, and the availability and quality of the equipment and materials.

With regard to the quality of learning attention is paid to: the degree of active involvement in the learning by the pupils and students; the range and balance of experience and attainment by individual pupils both across the curriculum and within subject areas; whether the tasks being undertaken are varied and include those which demand creative thought, along with those of practice; how the class-work is related to that undertaken outside school, for example at home, or on educational visits; whether the standards achieved by the pupils are commensurate with their abilities; whether work begun is usually completed; whether the pupils see the purpose of what they are doing; and whether they respond with enthusiasm and interest.

61

In coming to an evaluation of the teaching and learning, inspectors will also consider whether what is being taught is worth learning and take account of the extent to which teaching targets are being achieved in the learning. This criterion of the degree of match between that which is intended and that which is achieved is also relevant when looking at a department or school as a whole; for example in judging the extent to which the school has a set of aims which are reflected in the range of expertise possessed by the staff, the curriculum and associated schemes of work, the teaching methods, the pupils' attainments and the ways in which these are assessed. The extent to which such features match the policies of the local education authority also needs to be borne in mind.

In inspections of schools attention is also paid to whether the staffing is adequate for the school to carry out its tasks and to the efficiency and quality of leadership at all levels. Other criteria include whether the organisation provides satisfactory opportunities for children of all abilities: for example whether those with special needs are afforded reasonable opportunities to achieve the same broad educational aims as their peers; how the curricular aims and structure reflect the characteristics, elements and areas of learning and experience identified in discussion documents produced by the DES and HMI; the nature and extent of record keeping; whether the pupils are well cared for; the quality of relationships between teachers and pupils and between pupils and pupils; behaviour in class and about the school generally; discipline, both policy and practice; levels of attendance; the number and range of clubs and societies; and the quality and nature of links between the school and parents and others in the community. HMI also comment on the overall standards attained and whether these are reasonable.

Gathering the evidence

The capacity for inspection to assist in achieving improvements in the system, or particular parts of it, is bound up with the confidence which those in the educational service and the general public have in the quality of the evidence provided and the objectivity of any judgements and advice based on it. Central to the Inspectorate's role is the acquisition of first-hand knowledge based on looking at the work done in the classrooms where the teaching and learning take place. To this end in the autumn of 1984 the evidence of visits in England to 4,572, 7,582 and 326 lessons in maintained primary, secondary and special schools respectively was used by the Inspectorate in preparing its report on the effects of local authority expenditure policies on education provision[1].

---

[1] *Report by Her Majesty's Inspectors on the Effects of Local Authority Expenditure Policies on Education Provision in England — 1984*. DES, 1985.

Prior to being inspected it is usual for the school to be asked to provide a substantial amount of information which is studied by members of the inspection team. Such preparation is essential if time is not to be wasted during the inspection itself and it is in considering this initial information that each member of the team will identify certain questions for resolution, and hypotheses for confirmation or rejection, during the visit.

In coming to a considered view of the work in a subject department an inspector is interested especially in the aims and content of courses; the qualifications, training, experience and deployment of the staff; the accommodation and other resources being used; the quality of the teaching; and especially the response from the pupils. In gathering the evidence for this the inspector would need to attend a representative selection of lessons, hold discussions with staff, especially with the teacher in charge of the subject, and with pupils and students, study the evidence of written and practical work produced over a period of time by the pupils, and look at the premises and resources. In some inspections it may also be necessary to visit pupils who are off site, for example on work experience or undertaking field-work.

A full inspection also involves the panel of inspectors coming to an agreed view on the more general aspects of the school, such as the leadership, the management of resources, the extent to which the overall aims and objectives are being implemented, the coherence of the curricular policy, the quality of the pastoral support, teaching styles, the response from pupils and the general ethos and environment. It is the reporting inspector's responsibility, by discussion with the whole panel, to elicit generally agreed views on such issues and by the fourth day of an inspection the team would have a substantial amount of evidence on which to do this, including that provided by visits to perhaps 150 or more lessons in a large secondary school and by more than one visit to all the classes in a primary school.

The documentation used during an inspection will vary according to the nature of the exercise and the preference of individuals, but there is a substantial degree of common practice. Records for the working files on schools, for example, are written to a common format, surveys are supported by *aides-mémoire* to enable information to be gathered and retrieved systematically, and major surveys require the use of schedules of standard questions to be completed by HMI and sometimes also by the LEA or institution visited. Some exercises involve HMI in the completion of lesson observation schedules but it is not the Inspectorate's practice to use externally devised lists to tick off, total, and on that basis decide, what is good, bad or indifferent. In communicating a judgement HMI also use a variety of techniques, written prose is the most common, but some exercises require the use of gradings. This is especially the case with large, centrally arranged projects and where the data is to be processed by computer.

HMIs' main concern is to report on the standards of learning achieved and, along with the evidence of what is seen and heard, they make use of whatever objective measures of standards are to hand, such as the results of tests in literacy or numeracy, and the proportion of pupils or students entering for, and being successful in, public examinations. But during the inspection process countless judgements are made by individual inspectors which in the final analysis are subjective and depend essentially on the skill of the inspector in knowing what to look for, what to ask about and what to make of the evidence. In coming to such professional judgements the inspectors' expectations will be influenced by their experience as teachers, by what they have seen and know to be achievable in a broad range of similar schools elsewhere, and by collective discussion.

There are, of course, shortcomings in such practices. There is a limit to how much HMI can know directly of what takes place. The evidence of what occurred the week before, or the lesson before HMI arrived, is inevitably limited, if it exists at all. To assess the quality in some activities it is necessary to be there when they happen, such is the transitory nature of some of the work inspected. It is thus not always possible to verify whether a judgement is reasonable or not, but by talking to teachers and pupils, by looking at written work and by noting the ways in which pupils and teachers have established habits and styles, it is possible to minimise such risks. Ultimately, those who are inspected and reported on should feel that the inspectors are describing and commenting on a world which they recognise and know: that with all its shortcomings the institution, LEA or course at the centre of the report is recognisable to them and the judgements are broadly reasonable and fair.

Reporting

It is the duty of HMI to report as they find, not as others might wish them to find and not in the light of some secret blueprint known only to the inspectors. During and after an inspection of a school HMI discuss their findings with the head and those teachers who have responsibility for the areas inspected. Shortly after a full inspection HMI also offer to meet the governors of the school and they may also discuss their findings with LEA officers and advisers. Thereafter a report is written for the Secretary of State and much care is taken in its drafting, to ensure not only that it is factually accurate, but also that the whole panel is in agreement with the main evaluative comments, the reliability of which is thereby enhanced. The procedures for the inspection of independent schools are similar to those for the maintained sector.

HMI seek to define quality as they inspect and in reporting attempt to give a balanced picture, providing description as well as evaluation, and commendation as well as criticism. Since January 1983 reports to

the Secretary of State on formal inspections have been published by
him and thereby available to the public so that HMI's opinions,
although given only in relation to a selection of institutions, can be
broadly known and their applicability to other institutions considered
by a wide readership. Indeed, much of what the Inspectorate does and
says is now subject to public scrutiny, especially publications such as
the annual reports on the effects of local authority expenditure policies
on educational provision. At a local level a report of an inspection of a
school is likely to be a lively issue in a town, village or community.

The communication of findings, however, is only the beginning. For
improvement to follow inspection it is necessary for those with direct
responsibility for education — teachers, LEAs and governing bodies
— to consider the reports and to commit themselves to action. To seek
to ensure that there is effective action following published reports the
Secretary of State has introduced systematic procedures with LEAs
and governing bodies and statutory arrangements exist in respect of
independent schools. These procedures are the direct responsibility of
branches of the DES and not of the Inspectorate. Less formal follow-
up to an inspection may take a variety of forms, such as a return visit
by the general inspector for the institution some time after the
inspection, or specifically arranged follow-up work by various specialist
inspectors.

ANNEX

The Role of Her Majesty's Inspectorate

Her Majesty's Inspectorate was established in 1839 but the statutory basis of
the Inspectorate's current work is Section 77 of the Education Act 1944
which requires the Secretary of State to cause inspections to be made of
every educational establishment at such intervals as appear to be appropriate.
The Act also provides for inspectors to be appointed by HM The Queen on
the recommendation of the Minister.

The men and women who become HMI are recruited from those who have
had successful experience as teachers or lecturers. Some may also have been
advisers with local education authorities and many, particularly those
involved in the inspection of post-school education, have worked in industry
or commerce. All of them are specialists. For example, there are inspectors
whose knowledge and experience are in a particular phase of education, or in
a particular subject, and there are some whose interests and expertise lie
especially in the teaching of children or young people with special needs.

HM Inspectors (HMI) have a right in law to inspect almost all educational
institutions, both public and private, although they do not inspect the
universities, other than by visiting in respect of teacher training and extra
mural studies, nor do they inspect religious education in some
denominational schools. In addition, HMI have duties in relation to a large
number of other bodies; for example they inspect and report on the

education provided in hospitals and prisons, and on occasions work with officers in other government departments.

The role of HM Inspectorate is, first, to assess standards and trends and to advise the Secretary of State on the performance of the system, thereby helping the Government in the discharge of its duties. Under our decentralised system of government much of the responsibility for the provision of education rests with LEAs and the governors of schools, and the second part of the Inspectorate's role is to give judgements and advice to these bodies so that they may take constructive action. Thirdly, HMI seeks to contribute to the improvement of standards; for example by identifying and making more widely known good practices and promising developments, besides referring to weaknesses requiring attention.

HM Inspectorate has no legal powers of enforcement and no function which is independent of that of the Secretary of State. Its main role relates to central government and a substantial and increased proportion of its work is concerned with the outcomes of government policy. The decision to publish what HMI writes also rests with the Government. But the Inspectorate has an established professional independence in that, for example, anything which is published is as HMI has written it, and it is for the Inspectorate to decide how to go about the business of inspection and what to inspect. Moreover, in their relationships with education authorities and the profession generally, HMI takes an independent stance in judging the quality of education.

The Work of the Inspectorate

At 1 January 1984 there were 388 full-time HMI in post in England and the Secretary of State has approved a phased expansion of the Inspectorate to 490 by April 1988. The inspectors' remit includes over 28,000 maintained and independent schools and more than 1,000 establishments of further and higher education. HM Inspectorate is also involved in a wide range of activities within the education service; for example in district work in LEAs, in in-service training and in the work of examination boards and other groups, all of which helps to keep HMI informed of developments, trends and issues.

Because of the size and diversity of the system, however, and the size of the Inspectorate itself, there is a limit to what HMI can know directly of the service as a whole. It is not possible to do more than sample and the inspection programme has to be based on closely defined priorities. The scale and type of the inspections mounted are determined partly by the needs of the Secretary of State and the DES in discharging their responsibilities and partly by the need for the Inspectorate to monitor the system to seek to ensure that the quality of education is maintained. Thus the inspection programme reflects a balance between activities which are policy driven, those which will provide a national overview of the general quality of education, those which look at special aspects (for example at the work in subjects of the curriculum), and those which are territorially based, for example in particular local authorities. Furthermore, in their work HMI cannot confine themselves solely to inspections which arise from issues of the moment for they must also be concerned with identifying trends and developments within the system as a whole so that if the issues of the day change the evidence upon which to base opinion and advice is available.

HMI are invited to comment on a wide range of issues and sometimes an inspector is asked for an opinion in a field in which he or she has no special expertise but has access to guidance from specialist committees of HMI and colleagues. Indeed, the means by which the Inspectorate is itself kept up to date and informed are crucial to ensuring that the quality of advice given reflects views which are considered and broadly held.

Assessment Techniques and Approaches

2.6 Techniques for Appraising Teacher Performance

Paper by the Department of Education and Science

So important is high quality teaching to the delivery of good education that it would be impossible to run an effective school system without appraising the performance of teachers. Teachers are appraised daily in the schools of England and Wales. Current practice is characterised by its informality, the virtual absence of any articulated theory, and the general lack of system. Teachers are not always sure how or when appraisal takes place. But it does and its results can be seen in the aggregation of the multiple judgmental and developmental decisions which underpin the current distribution and disposition of the teacher force; for example:

— the arrangement of the 415,000 full-time teachers into 27,000 heads (7 per cent), 30,000 deputies (7 per cent), 7,000 senior teachers (2 per cent), 29,000 Scale 4 teachers (7 per cent), 70,000 Scale 3 teachers (17 per cent), 130,000 Scale 2 teachers (31 per cent) and 121,000 Scale 1 teachers (29 per cent);

— turnover whereby, for example, in 1983–84 about 32,000 full-time teachers (7.6 per cent) transferred to different posts in different schools;

— latest figures suggest that approximately 7,000 full-time equivalent teachers, or 1.7 per cent of the teacher force, were released from normal teaching duties to attend in-service training courses in 1984–85. We cannot say precisely how many actual teachers benefited: data from a 1982–83 survey would suggest that in excess of 250,000 individual teacher secondments, of whatever length, are involved.

The current arrangements are not ideal but they deliver. The question is whether the appraisal techniques now in use can be bettered. This paper concedes the impossibility of a perfect system of appraisal and considers what techniques are available and how they might be used to produce a system in which imperfections would be explicitly recognised and attempts made to minimise their effects.

The following list of the frequently cited characteristics for acceptable forms of appraisal is not comprehensive — developmental, supportive, non-threatening, positive, objective, fair, free of bias, consistent, open to scrutiny, professionally prepared and agreed, adequately resourced and sufficiently well endowed to facilitate follow-up action (for example, INSET) and comprehensive training for appraisers and appraisees alike — but it indicates the nature and complexity of any desirable system.

These are real difficulties. For example it is argued that:

— there is no unambiguous educational output which can be measured and attributed to the individual teacher;

— it is not possible to build up from discrete aspects of performance to an assessment of the overall effectiveness of the teacher;

— it is very difficult to operate multi-purpose appraisal so that it bears simultaneously and equally effectively upon decisions relating to professional performance on the one hand and career development and potential on the other. (In the jargon, 'formative' and 'summative' approaches are best kept separate and distinct. Otherwise role conflict will occur, with the appraiser unable to reconcile the functions of performance improvement/professional development and personnel management.)

Teacher appraisal involves three closely related processes:

    i. agreeing what is expected of the teacher—

       a. a job specification

       b. criteria for appraising performance in the job

   ii. collecting evidence on the teacher's performance

  iii. making judgments, reaching decisions and acting upon them.

These are considered in turn.

Agreeing expectations

The job specification or job description needs to be drawn up with care. There is a risk of specifications which elaborate all the non-teaching tasks without making clear the central teaching function. Specifications with the right teaching orientation will provide a better indication of the relative weight to be attached to the various responsibilities of particular posts. It is important to remember the wide range of jobs covered by the generic term, teaching — for example, infant class teacher for six year-olds; upper secondary classics teacher; middle school PE teacher specialising in games; secondary music teacher specialising in individual and group work in string playing. The job description should focus on the specific teaching function. It might also be supplemented periodically by specific post-related goals or targets. Precision and clarity are essential — as is dynamism: it is important that job descriptions should be updated to reflect changes of function, emphasis or priority.

Research has not unearthed any simple or comprehensive indicator of effective teacher performance. Commonsense observation reveals clearly good and clearly bad teachers. While it is not obvious that there are any appraisal criteria which can readily resolve this apparent paradox, it does seem possible to reduce the problems associated with appraising a multi-purpose activity such as teaching, which is directed towards a varied clientele under variable conditions and in accordance with varied curricular approaches according to different authority and school policies. Certain major factors must be controlled before any attempt can be made to judge whether individual teachers are effective. For a start they all work in schools, institutions with distinctive characteristics, managements and policies, all of which have a major bearing on the individual teacher's performance. Then the characteristics of the pupil population (age, ability, aptitude and mix) must be registered so that what is under consideration is 'value-added' rather than 'end-value', much of which lies beyond the short-run control of the individual teacher. This control of the 'raw material' must be accompanied by some form of controlling or at least disciplining the subjectivity of the appraiser.

In the USA the general approach to appraisal has been to build up from discrete competencies through to overall effectiveness. This process has usefully been summarised as follows:

> 'TEACHER COMPETENCY refers to any single knowledge, skill, or professional value position, which is relevant to successful teaching practice. Competencies refer to specific things that teachers know, do, or believe, but not to the effects of these attributes on others.
>
> TEACHER COMPETENCE refers to the repertoire of competencies a teacher possesses. Overall competence is a matter of the degree to which a teacher has mastered a set of individual competencies, some of which are more critical than others.
>
> TEACHER PERFORMANCE refers to what a teacher does on the job rather than to what he or she can do. Teacher performance is specific to the job situation; it depends on the competence of the teacher, the context in which the teacher works, and the teacher's ability to apply his or her competencies at any time.
>
> TEACHER EFFECTIVENESS refers to the effect that a teacher's performance has on pupils. Teacher effectiveness depends not only on competence and performance but also on the response pupils make. Just as competence cannot always predict performance, teacher performance does not automatically lead to intended outcomes.'

In Georgia, 16 competencies have been identified (see Annex, page 74). By way of illustration, the criterion of communication with pupils is specified as follows:

'COMPETENCY VII — COMMUNICATES WITH LEARNERS

Indicator 4   Gives directions and explanations related to lesson content

Indicator 5   Clarifies directions and explanations when learners misunderstand lesson content

Indicator 6   Uses responses and questions from learners in teaching

Indicator 7   Provides feedback to learners throughout the lesson

Indicator 8   Uses acceptable written and oral expression with learners[1]'

While such task-related criteria seem a distinct advance on personality-related criteria (the 'trait-rating' approach in which teachers are appraised against the possession of qualities judged significant for effective performance as a teacher), problems remain. Comprehensive lists grow long with the attendant risk of distorted teaching approaches as teachers endeavour to accommodate appraisal competencies by resorting to safe, didactic and unimaginative teaching. It is vital that these problems be considered during the criterion selection process to ensure that appraisal enables sound judgments to be made and so that appraisal supports rather than inhibits good teaching practice.

Collecting evidence

The next problem is to establish sound procedures for determining whether teachers satisfy the agreed criteria. The most important decisions are the type of information to be used (in particular whether it is performance or outcomes that are to be studied) and by whom is to be gathered. There would seem to be six possible approaches, some of which could be used in combination with others. What is intended is that all teachers, including headteachers, should be embraced by the appraisal system.

a. SUPERORDINATE APPRAISAL, operated by the teachers themselves in the schools, but overseen and monitored by LEA management using the expertise of their advisory services, might well entail a continuing and evolutionary process in which the two trained teachers meet on a regular basis for a preparatory, structured interview prior to one or more pre-arranged and unannounced observation periods followed by a further interview to discuss strengths and weaknesses, explore needs, and set goals. The formal results of the appraisal, set out in an open written report and specifying the appraisal criteria and their indicators, can be relayed at this interview or it can be done by the teacher or officer responsible for monitoring and moderating the superordinate's appraisal. The difficulties are evident. A great deal rests upon adequate interviewing and narrative appraisal skills. Classroom observation is widely regarded as the best means of appraising teacher performance. Teaching in the classroom is the essence of the job. But its success depends upon proper lesson

---

[1] Medley D M (1984). 'Teacher Competency' in Cresap, McCormick and Page. *Teacher Incentives — A Tool for Effective Management*. Reston (Virginia): National Association of Secondary School Principals.

preparation and effective marking to reinforce what is delivered in the classroom. Are these activities to be appraised through observation, their carry-through and effect upon lessons to be implied by the skilled observer? And who is to observe, for how long and how often, and using what sort of instruments? Is the superordinate (who may not command the necessary subject specialism for example) the best observer, or should there be multiple observers who, as well as providing the specialist and generalist mix, would work against single observer bias? How frequent must the observations be to provide a solid sample of classroom performance to avoid judgments based on atypical lessons? How are reliability and consistency to be assured? Can such instruments as behaviourally anchored rating scales (BARS) find a place in the schools of England and Wales, or are there to be other more pragmatic ways of controlling the subjectivity of the observer? Certainly it is important that observation for appraisal purposes should not exclude observers from being able to commend and reinforce good practice ('catch them being good' etc) and assist in improvements.

b. PEER APPRAISAL* might follow a largely similar pattern of interview/ observation/dialogue, but this approach also lends itself to descriptive documentation with the appraisee submitting work objectives and samples (eg. course outline, objectives, role in the curriculum, course delivery, assessment and marking of pupils) for appraisal of teaching competence and suggestions for improvement. It is extremely difficult to conceive of personnel decisions being based solely upon findings derived from peer appraisal. Involving teachers in appraising their peers encourages professionalism, provides greater variety to teaching work, reduces the isolation teachers feel in their classrooms, and supports the exchange of knowledge. Peer appraisal seems best suited for use in improving teacher performance.

c. SELF-APPRAISAL is often seen as the desirable preliminary to external appraisal along the lines of a. or b.; of itself — even with a common checklist or prompt sheet — it must be a solitary exercise. Though it is undoubtedly valuable for teachers to review their responsibilities, aims, objectives, results and professional development, the absence of any external validation can leave the exercise in a vacuum. It may be possible to overcome this to some extent by standardising the process and subjecting it to external monitoring with managers holding teachers accountable for their plans of self-appraisal. The evidence is inconclusive. Some studies suggest that self-appraisers are too hard on themselves, others that they overrate themselves. As with b. it is difficult to conceive of this option being used other than for purposes of improvement.

d. SUBORDINATE APPRAISAL might have a part to play in analysing the performance of school heads and LEA managers. A recent initiative in Dekalb County, Georgia, would seem to merit consideration. Appraisal is done by the staff of the school, by a superior officer of the County staff and by the head himself. The results are normed on those for the total number of schools and expressed as a percentage of

---

* As some commentators use peer appraisal to mean appraisal by fellow teachers it is necessary to say that what is meant here is appraisal by teaching colleagues at the same level of responsibility.

positive responses on each competency. Each head receives a print-out which shows, against each competency, the number of observations by his staff against the average county wide, plus those of his superior officer and himself. The three-point profile provides the head with a view of his position in relation to others in the county, and gives him some useful indications of his or her professional development needs.

e. PUPIL ACHIEVEMENT provides the most direct evidence of teaching effectiveness as well as the evidence most prone to misinterpretation. The ultimate test of a teacher is the student learning produced. Teachers need accurate information about what their pupils are learning if they are to improve their teaching. But the effects of teachers on different groups of students are relatively inconsistent over time; these effects are even unstable from one topic to another for the same students. Moreover there is the risk that teachers may teach to the test or may direct their attention only to those pupils who are likely to show the greatest gains in achievement.

f. PUPIL RATINGS have been tried in the USA where research provides strong empirical support that college student ratings are highly stable, strongly related to student achievement and are highly effective in promoting improvement within a class. This research suggests that student ratings represent a sound choice for evaluating instruction at the US college level. Such ratings can provide crucial information on student satisfaction, on attitudes to professional obligations and on specific course or lesson components. It is highly unlikely that this option can possibly cross the cultural gap from US colleges (and to some extent schools) to schools in England and Wales.

Making judgements and acting upon them

With expectations clear and evidence gathered, the evidence must be weighed to inform the judgements and decisions within schools and across LEAs which need to be taken to improve teacher performance and to provide the most effective management of the teacher force. Amongst the range of possible actions and outcomes arising might be listed:

— modified behaviour/approach by the teacher;

— presentation of opportunities/experiences (eg. visits, observation of others' lessons, secondments) for further and better-informed staff development;

— training opportunities, be they in-school or outside;

— change of posting to widen or deepen experience, or to give a better match of teacher to task;

— a new, up-to-date information base on teacher performance for the use of LEAs and governing bodies, facilitating better deployment of staff, improved personnel management and better managed schools.

This list would seem to justify the undoubted effort which needs to be put into designing and launching a systematic approach to appraisal. The overall outcome should be better decisions feeding through to better management, better teacher performance and better pupil achievement. This intended outcome must be carefully monitored and empirical study will be needed of the relationship between appraisal and the standards it is intended to raise.

ANNEX

COMPETENCIES AND INDICATORS

COMPETENCY I:	*PLANS INSTRUCTION TO ACHIEVE OBJECTIVES*
Indicator 1	Specifies or selects learner objectives for lessons
Indicator 2	Specifies or selects teaching procedures for lessons
Indicator 3	Specifies or selects content, materials, and media for lessons
Indicator 4	Specifies or selects materials and procedures for assessing learner progress on the objectives
Indicator 5	Plans instruction at a variety of levels
COMPETENCY II:	*ORGANISES INSTRUCTION TO TAKE INTO ACCOUNT INDIVIDUAL DIFFERENCES AMONG LEARNERS*
Indicator 6	Organises instruction to take into account differences among learners in their capabilities
Indicator 7	Organises instruction to take into account differences among learners in their learning style
Indicator 8	Organises instruction to take into account differences among learners in their rates of learning
COMPETENCY III:	*OBTAINS AND USES INFORMATION ABOUT THE NEEDS AND PROGRESS OF INDIVIDUAL LEARNERS*
Indicator 9	Uses teacher-made or teacher-selected evaluation materials or procedures to obtain information about learner progress
Indicator 10	Communicates with individual learners about their needs and progress

COMPETENCY IV: *REFERS LEARNERS WITH SPECIAL PROBLEMS TO SPECIALISTS*

Indicator 11   Obtains and uses information about learners from cumulative records

Indicator 12   Identifies learners who require the assistance of specialists

Indicator 13   Obtains and uses information from co-workers and parents to assist with specific learner problems

COMPETENCY V: *OBTAINS AND USES INFORMATION ABOUT THE EFFECTIVENESS OF INSTRUCTION TO REVISE IT WHEN NECESSARY*

Indicator 14   Obtains information on the effectiveness of instruction

Indicator 15   Revises instruction as needed using evaluation results and observation data

COMPETENCY VI: *USES INSTRUCTIONAL TECHNIQUES, METHODS AND MEDIA-RELATED TO THE OBJECTIVES*

Indicator 1   Uses teaching methods appropriate for objectives, learners and environment

Indicator 2   Uses instructional equipment and other instructional aids

Indicator 3   Uses instructional materials that provide learners with appropriate practice on objectives

COMPETENCY VII: *COMMUNICATES WITH LEARNERS*

Indicator 4   Gives directions and explanations related to lesson content

Indicator 5   Clarifies directions and explanations when learners misunderstand lesson content

Indicator 6   Uses responses and questions from learners in teaching

Indicator 7   Provides feedback to learners throughout the lesson

Indicator 8   Uses acceptable written and oral expression with learners

COMPETENCY VIII: *DEMONSTRATES A REPERTOIRE OF TEACHING METHODS*

Indicator 9   Implements learning activities in a logical sequence

Indicator 10   Demonstrates ability to conduct lessons using a variety of teaching methods

Indicator 11   Demonstrates ability to work with individuals, small groups, and large groups

COMPETENCY IX: *REINFORCES AND ENCOURAGES LEARNER INVOLVEMENT IN INSTRUCTION*

Indicator 12   Uses procedures which get learners initially involved in lessons

Indicator 13   Provides learners with opportunities for participating

Indicator 14   Maintains learner involvement in lessons

Indicator 15   Reinforces and encourages the efforts of learners to maintain involvement

COMPETENCY X: *DEMONSTRATES AN UNDERSTANDING OF THE SCHOOL SUBJECT BEING TAUGHT*

Indicator 16   Helps learners recognize the purpose and importance of topics or activities

Indicator 17   Demonstrates knowledge in the subject area

COMPETENCY XI: *ORGANISES TIME, SPACE, MATERIALS AND EQUIPMENT FOR INSTRUCTION*

Indicator 18   Attends to routine tasks

Indicator 19   Uses instructional time effectively

Indicator 20   Provides a learning environment that is attractive and orderly

COMPETENCY XII: *DEMONSTRATES ENTHUSIASM FOR TEACHING AND LEARNING AND THE SUBJECT BEING TAUGHT*

Indicator 1   Communicates personal enthusiasm

Indicator 2   Stimulates learner interest

Indicator 3   Conveys the impression of knowing what to do and how to do it

COMPETENCY XIII: *HELPS LEARNERS DEVELOP POSITIVE SELF-CONCEPTS*

Indicator 4   Demonstrates warmth and friendliness

Indicator 5   Demonstrates sensitivity to the needs and feelings of learners

Indicator 6   Demonstrates patience, empathy and understanding

COMPETENCY XIV: *MANAGES CLASSROOM INTERACTIONS*

Indicator 7   Provides feedback to learners about their behaviour

Indicator 8   Promotes comfortable interpersonal relationships

Indicator 9   Maintains appropriate classroom behaviour

Indicator 10   Manages disruptive behaviour among learners

COMPETENCY XV:	*MEETS PROFESSIONAL RESPONSIBILITIES*
Indicator 1	Work co-operatively with colleagues, administrators and community members
Indicator 2	Follows the policies and procedures of the school district
Indicator 3	Demonstrates ethical behaviour
Indicator 4	Performs extra-instructional duties
COMPETENCY XVI:	*ENGAGES IN PROFESSIONAL SELF-DEVELOPMENT*
Indicator 5	Participates in professional growth activities
Indicator 6	Shares and seeks professional materials and ideas

Assessment Techniques and Approaches

2.7 School Self-evaluation

Paper by Her Majesty's Inspectorate

In recent years the education service has become increasingly aware of the need to ensure that the education being provided in our schools is appropriate and relevant to the present and future needs of young people. At the same time, the community outside the school is seeking more assurance of the quality of that provision.

Attention has focused on the four principal components of educational provision: curriculum, teachers and teaching, organisation, and resources; although the various interest groups have different perspectives and emphases.

Various initiatives, such as the HMI/LEA 11–16 Curriculum exercise[1] conducted in five LEAs from 1977 to 1982 and DES circulars 6/81[2] and 8/83[3] (which required LEAs to define their curriculum policies and to show how they were being implemented) encouraged both schools and LEAs to review and evaluate their curricula. Many chose to do so by means of various self-evaluation schemes.

Further pressure to re-examine the curriculum and the delivery of that curriculum is being provided by continuing government interest, indicated by the recent publication of the White Paper *Better Schools*, as well as by the current HMI 'Curriculum Matters' series. Another influence has been the increasing interest in vocational and pre-vocational education, the involvement of the Manpower Services Commission (MSC) and the introduction of the Technical and Vocational Education Initiative (TVEI).

The introduction of comprehensive education in the sixties and seventies gave rise to larger and more complex secondary schools and the consequent need for more sophisticated organisation and management — points which were later reinforced by the HMI primary and secondary surveys[4, 5]. Management courses for heads

---

[1] DES. *Curriculum 11–16: a Review of Progress.* A joint study by HMI and five LEAs. HMSO, 1981. (Interim report.) *Curriculum 11–16. Towards a statement of entitlement.* Curricular appraisal in action. HMSO, 1983.

[2] *The School Curriculum* (Circular 6/81). DES, 1981.

[3] *The School Curriculum.* (Circular 8/83). DES, 1983.

[4] DES. *Primary Education in England.* A survey by HMI. HMSO, 1978 (repr. with corrections 1981).

[5] DES. *Aspects of Secondary Education in England.* A survey by HMI. HMSO, 1979.

emphasised the idea of the school as an organisation and the head as a manager and leader. At least partly as a result of these influences, there has been a change in management style in recent years, with less emphasis on autocratic leadership and more on consultation and debate. The result has been more open discussion in schools before decisions are taken and a more structured approach to change. These conditions have both encouraged evaluation and constituted part of the evaluation process.

The coincidence of falling rolls and national economic recession have brought an urgent need for change at a time when limited resources are available and have accelerated the desirability of evaluating the performance of schools as organisations. There are other demands for greater accountability. There is the belief that schools should be more accountable to the users of education — pupils, parents, the community and industry — not only for the efficiency of the organisation but for the nature and quality of the education being offered and the learning being achieved.

Falling rolls require schools to review the curriculum and the teachers themselves need clear staff development policies, perhaps based in part on appraisal, if they are to be equipped for changing roles, maintain morale and achieve career enhancement.

By 1984, well over half the LEAs in England had instituted their own schemes of school evaluation or were supporting and encouraging individual school initiatives. In the main, LEA schemes are concerned with school organisation, curriculum and resources. Until recently, they have been reluctant to propose systematic teacher appraisal; but now a few of them are making progress in this area. Developments in individual schools run parallel to LEA initiatives. The emphasis is mainly on the curriculum, its organisation and implementation. A number, and among them the most successful schemes, combine both institutional evaluation of systems, processes and outcomes and staff appraisal/development.

A number of terms recur frequently in LEA and school documentation: eg. appraisal, assessment, evaluation and review. There is, however, some inconsistency in the ways these terms are used. For the purpose of this paper the following distinctions are made:

i.   evaluation is a general term used to describe any activity by the institution or the LEA where the quality of the provision is the subject of systematic study;

ii. review indicates a retrospective activity and implies the collection and examination of evidence and information;

iii. appraisal emphasises the forming of qualitative judgements about an activity, a person or an organisation;

    iv. assessment implies the use of measurement and/or grading based on known criteria.

Purposes

The prime purpose of individual schools, both primary and secondary, undertaking self-evaluation is to improve the quality of the pupils' learning and the functioning of the schools. For the most part it is not in response to perceived problems but is seen as a professional responsibility. Few schools reject the notion of accountability, though for some it is seen as being accountable not so much to the LEA as to the pupils, the parents and the community.

LEA schemes also stress improvement as the major objective and, like the schools, assume the process is valuable in itself. The relationship between self-evaluation and accountability is not always clearly and explicitly defined. One LEA at least was prompted initially by demands for greater accountability but has since shifted the emphasis more towards the developmental role of evaluation. Where full written reports are required by LEAs, then schools tend to see the main function of the exercise as accountability and regard the writing of the report as the main task to be accomplished rather than a preliminary to action and further evaluation.

Scope

Determining the scope of any exercise is a crucial preliminary stage and heads have a key role in explaining the purposes and nature of the exercise to their staff. It is equally important to involve all teachers in the initial process of establishing an order of priority of areas to be considered. A realistic scale should be set to the exercise, so that efforts are concentrated on a number of key areas where there is a likelihood of positive results within a reasonable period of time. One national scheme, Guidelines for Review and Internal Development in Schools (GRIDS), has this process built in. Commitment is greatest where teachers are involved in this way. Failing to do so is often associated with confusion as to the purpose, a loss of impetus and uneven results. A major drawback of the LEA schemes requiring evaluation of all areas of school life for a formal report is that the teachers' efforts are dissipated by trying to cover too much ground.

There is a tendency for primary schools to look particularly at curriculum issues, most frequently specific subject areas. In secondary schools there is more emphasis on management and organisation reflecting the greater structural complexity of these institutions. Discussion of the curriculum tends to concentrate on the nature of the provision, on questions of balance and the introduction of new courses. There is, however, evidence that some schools are beginning to look at the effect of their policies on pupils' learning; but observation of classroom activity remains rare. It is difficult to see how such self-evaluation can be truly effective unless the processes of the teaching and learning and the outcomes in terms of pupils' responses are given at least as close a scrutiny as the inputs of provision. Similarly, little attention is paid to the legitimate interests and influences of those outside the school in most self-evaluative procedures. Parents, governors, LEA officials and members and the wider community might usefully contribute more to school evaluation.

Methods

Evaluation schemes vary considerably in their structure but there appear to be two distinct approaches. Formal LEA schemes tend to have detailed schedules of questions to be answered by schools across the whole range of their activity. The second approach is to identify some topics of particular concern to the school and to focus on these. Within this category, schools following the GRIDS scheme have particular procedures to follow which they apply to the areas under review: an initial review to identify priorities is followed by specific reviews, with detailed guidance for the collection and evaluation of evidence, and an implementation of recommendations. Many individual schools follow this general approach, though often with a less detailed and coherent structure.

The most usual method of proceeding is by the use of working parties. In primary schools it is common for teachers to volunteer to join groups that interest them. Such groups are often led by subject co-ordinators. In the smallest schools topics may be tackled by the whole staff, often by discussion. In the secondary schools little is done on a whole school basis. Working parties are usually established on a subject or pastoral basis. For more general topics the working parties are usually drawn from a number of subject disciplines, interest groups and levels of seniority.

Proceedings in small schools are often informal, making use of whole staff discussions. In larger schools, and particularly in secondary schools, where communication might be more problematic, proceedings are usually formal with minutes on meetings kept and circulated to all staff. In larger schools in particular it is important that there is a commonly agreed purpose and structure to which all activity relates, and monitoring by the senior management of the school to ensure that the direction and the momentum of the work is maintained.

Many LEA schemes require the collection of large amounts of factual information and description. These demands can pre-occupy the schools' response and obscure those questions which require an evaluative judgement. On the other hand, not all schools are aware of the need to have an adequate information base in order to make reliable judgements. There is a tendency for some to move directly from identifying an area of concern to the formulation of a new policy, without first thoroughly analysing the problem, thus breaking the logical sequence of data collection, testing hypotheses and making value judgements.

Criteria

Although all schemes, whether LEA or individual, are involved, to a greater or lesser extent, in making judgements about quality and effectiveness it is a difficult task to articulate criteria of quality which will be acceptable to all, and few of them, as yet, have clear and explicit statements. Values are implied in some of the questions asked in formal schemes and a few schools have general criteria (very few with matching departmental criteria): but in general, some kind of consensus is assumed. This may be a reality in, for example, small primary schools where teachers in regular close contact discuss the quality of work produced; but in larger schools the assumption of a consensus on this basis is to a greater or lesser extent illusory. Yet only when criteria are identified and agreed is it likely that the teaching and learning throughout a school can become effectively focused and co-ordinated.

External support

Schools operating evaluation schemes do so with less external involvement than might be expected; although in a few cases there is a fruitful collaboration with the staff of institutes of higher education and other 'critical friends'. There is almost no involvement of parents or governors in the process except as recipients of reports in some cases. What involvement there is from outside the schools comes chiefly from LEA advisers and inspectors. In LEA schemes they are usually involved in initial briefings and in reporting-back sessions; otherwise, with a few notable exceptions, their role in schools' self-evaluation is limited to providing encouragement. In a few authorities advisers/inspectors are required to validate the school's own self-evaluation or to conduct a joint evaluation with the school. There are indications that the current level and nature of advisory provision might not be sufficient to provide greater help than at present without some drastic re-ordering of priorities, but external support is almost always helpful and frequently provides the impetus to get the evaluation off the grounds. It should, of course, be added that many LEA advisers/inspectors are required to evaluate schools themselves by means of formal and informal inspection.

Reporting

Schools producing written reports covering all aspects of their self-evaluation are usually required to do so by their LEA. The full reports which are produced are generally long and contain a high proportion of description of organisation and structures and relatively little evaluation. There is rarely much reference to classroom practice or to pupil outcomes other than examination results. In general, the issues which emerge relate to resources, organisation and curriculum planning. Although schools operating their own schemes do not generally produce full written reports, most produce internal papers, recommendations, plans and structures for their own use; in some cases they are sent to LEAs and governors. In primary schools they most frequently take the form of revised subject guidelines, aimed at bringing about improvements in pupils' learning. The papers produced in secondary schools tend to be of two kinds: revised schemes of work and working party papers containing mainly a description of present practices and detailed plans for the future.

Outcomes

In all schools evaluation is followed by some action and this is sometimes considerable. Some changes are organisational, other administrative, but the majority are concerned with the curriculum: in re-writing the school's aims and objectives; the introduction of new courses; the revision of schemes of work; the development of more sophisticated assessment and monitoring schemes. There remains a lack of emphasis on the actual processes and outcomes of the teaching and learning.

In-service education and training (INSET)

One notable result of evaluation activity has been the increased demand and need for INSET, both school-based and external. Schools need to ensure that before they become involved in evaluation, they are sufficiently well versed in the necessary techniques and have established a climate where it may succeed. The main demand is created as the school discovers areas where improvements are needed or new developments are desirable. Without the necessary INSET support at this stage, impetus is lost and disillusion sets in. A frequent criticism made by schools is of LEAs' inability to respond adequately to evaluation and to provide support for follow-up action and development. There are indications that the problems are being recognised. Some LEAs are tying INSET programmes to the needs identified by evaluation; for example, in one authority a scheme has been set up for short-term group secondments to look at specific problems. An LEA, where previously the main thrust had been towards accountability, has created a senior-level post to monitor evaluation and support developments. The demand on resources is considerable, even more so when one takes into account staff-appraisal schemes.

Monitoring

An essential feature of succesful evaluation activity is that the process should be monitored at all stages. There is evidence that review groups and subject departments encounter difficulties which could be overcome or avoided by more careful monitoring and appropriate action. It is particularly important at the stage of implementing recommendations.

Time

An important factor to be borne in mind in considering evaluation and the changes that may follow it is the time-scale involved. In practice, the majority of evaluation activities appear to take at least a year to reach even the implementation stage. This is particularly true for schools with little previous experience in carrying out evaluation. For these schools even more time may need to be spent before embarking on a project in establishing an appropriate school climate and acquiring the necessary skills. Even when the implementation stage has been reached, more time is required before the effectiveness of new initiatives can be measured. Curriculum developments especially may require several years before the effects are measurable in terms of pupil outcomes. The other aspect of time is the demand made on individual teachers. Almost all evaluation activity has to take place in addition to teaching and other school commitments. The burden is heaviest when the school is required to produce a full report within a limited time. This time and the effort spent have to be measured against the results of the exercise.

Effectiveness

In most schools it is too early for developments to have had observable effects in the classroom and to measure them reliably would require a longitudinal study. A considerable number of changes have been made which are potentially beneficial — changes to the curriculum, schemes of work and assessment — but very few which bear directly upon pupils' day-to-day classroom experiences.

The main claim made for self-evaluation is that it has increased the commitment, confidence and professionalism of the teachers involved, giving them a broader professional perspective and increasing their readiness and ability to examine critically what they are doing. If that is all, it is still very valuable, since these qualities are essential if improvements are to be made in the quality of the education received by children.

School self-evaluation can made a valuable contribution to the requirements of accountability. There are a number of steps which would have to be taken to ensure that such a contribution is effective:

a. LEAs should establish a clear policy framework within which school self-evaluation can operate (general encouragement is not enough). This would provide coherence, consistency and support.

b. Information gathering should be clearly separate from assessment and evaluation.

c. There should be less reliance on all-embracing schedules and more emphasis on providing procedures and a methodology which would allow priorities to be established for more detailed evaluation in an agreed number of areas, determined by the capacity of the school to carry them out thoroughly within a reasonable time span.

d. The LEA needs to provide support, expertise and, if necessary, outside consultants at all stages and to monitor the process.

e. Evaluation needs to be focused more on what goes on in classrooms and the pupil learning which is achieved.

f. Following upon evaluation the LEA has an important support role. INSET and other forms of professional development and perhaps resource needs will have been identified and must be addressed if schools and teachers are not to become disillusioned about the value of the exercise in securing improvement.

The Role and Responsibility of the School

3.0 An Overview

Peggy Marshall, CBE, formerly Chief Inspector for Secondary Education, HM Inspectorate

This session differs in one important respect from the two which follow. They consider the actions of local authorities and government in conducing to better schools. This session asks what can and should schools do to improve themselves — though not necessarily by themselves. LEAs and government and, less directly, other external forces act upon the schools, controlling, guiding, enabling, facilitating — or not, as the case may be. The schools are required also to act upon themselves, by the way they interpret their task, by the manner in which they operate and by the extent to which they are able to be honestly and constructively self-critical.

So, what is 'the school'? Leaving aside the bricks and mortar — though preferably not neglecting them too long or too much — it is a working community of teachers and pupils. Its achievements lie in the learning that takes place, both in the classroom and through the quality of life shared. The essential responsibility for the well-being of the school lies with the teachers. Central government, the LEA, the governors, the parents can inhibit or encourage, support or neglect; they can help create the conditions under which a school may better thrive, but they are not the school. In a vital sense, the teachers are, and when we ask 'the school' to address its responsibilities for appraisal and assessment, we are asking the teachers to engage in a difficult exercise in detached criticism, even while they must remain deeply involved in, and highly committed to, an institution which is larger than themselves.

It is not an unreasonable expectation of professional people. Whether they are actually able to do it effectively depends on other factors besides their own willingness. But most teachers would recognise and accept the direct responsibility for the quality of education in their school.

There is some encouraging evidence in the papers that follow, written by the Heads of two primary and two secondary schools. I do not propose, or presume, to summarise each of these papers, or to attempt fine textual comment. Taken together, the papers do provide illustrations of thoughtful policies in action, and indicate directions in which they, and other schools like them, are moving.

They offer starting points, some examples of success, and a few warning signals.

They show us schools engaged in a mixture of curriculum review, pupil assessment and teacher appraisal. They also confirm what commonsense and experience would suggest—that all these aspects of school evaluation are closely interconnected.

Assessment of the performance and the progress of the pupils must lead throughtful teachers to consider how far the content of the curriculum, and their own styles and methods of teaching, may be assisting or impeding that progress. In day-to-day work that kind of questioning is familiar to anyone who ever marked a set of exercise books, or scanned the latest list of examination results, and wondered...

But once a school seeks, as *Mrs Spaull* puts it, 'to make explicit what has always been implicit in a good school' by a systematic approach, then it has to bring together the efforts of all members of the staff into a more effectively co-ordinated whole. All the papers point to the need to clarify general aims and identify specific objectives; to establish coherent policies and modes of operation, and to create or strengthen management structures to support them.

The observation and analysis, consultation and discussion involved have themselves an educative value, and may constitute a major part of the school's own contribution to the training and development of the staff. It has, however, also to monitor its own endeavours and find ways of utilising the outcomes, both by changing practice within the school and by bringing to the attention of the LEA those needs, particularly for in-service training, which cannot be met by the individual school alone.

Effective follow-up, of whatever kind, is particularly important: any large-scale evaluation exercise is a great devourer of time and energies, and any such attempt which sinks without a trace in a sea of paper, or worse still, in a heap of computer printouts laden with more information than any reasonable person wishes to know, can only discourage future efforts.

The four papers differ usefully in a number of ways. The two primary schools are both concerned with selected aspects of the school's work. *Mr Taylor* describes a scheme for assessing all the key members of staff who hold posts of responsibility; *Mrs Spaull* describes a school already obliged by circumstances to embark on self-review, and moving to much more refined and structured evaluation of some selected aspects of the curriculum. Both, in their accounts of developments and reflections upon them, indicate how readily in one school curriculum evaluation led on to staff appraisal, and in the other staff appraisal, which included observation in the classroom, pointed up the needs for changes in schemes of work, in teaching methods and in the performance of the pupils.

The two secondary papers both offer general reflections on the place of assessment and appraisal in the functioning of schools, and illustrate the systems in operation in these schools. Neither claims to offer instant formulae for universal application, but they do speak from experience rather than theory.

As might be expected there are considerable differences of detailed practice as between primary and secondary schools, partly reflecting differences in size and relative complexity of organisation. All emphasise whole school involvement, but such involvement obviously carries different connotations in a primary school with 12 or 15 teachers, and in very much larger secondary schools with a hierarchy of senior staff and large subject departments. In the small primary school any major exercise willy nilly involves virtually everyone, and the direct demands on the head are heavy. In the large secondary school tasks can more readily be delegated and distributed, but more complex lines of communication and management structures have to be sustained, and establishing an overview of collective needs and collective achievements may be the more difficult.

There are other differences, arising from the ages of the pupils and the greater or lesser ease of contact with parents. Perhaps the most obvious difference of all lies in the fact that pupils reach the end of compulsory schooling in the secondary school, and the need for evidence of achievement, particularly performance in public examinations, creates a particular pressure not really paralleled in the primary school, except where rarely 11-plus selection lingers on.

But those differences aside, what comes through is an essential similarity of purpose and outcome.

The four papers indicate the various starting points for the schools concerned, and their underlying purposes. I quote:

1. (*Mrs Spaull*) 'The aims of evaluation and assessment are to improve pupil performances and understanding and enhance the quality of the teaching and learning process'. The related objectives included: 'to assess the school's needs and priorities for development' and 'to meet the professional development needs of teachers alongside the needs of the school'.

2. (*Mr Price*) on pupil assessment: 'We must not lose sight of the prime objective...the improvement of teacher: pupil relationships and an improvement in educational standards', and again. 'not only should assessment help to motivate pupil response...but it should also make a major contribution to the evaluation of the effectiveness and suitability of the courses being taught...'

3. (*Mr Taylor*)—with specific reference to a teacher appraisal system, 'it is designed...to ensure that each area of the curriculum is successfully planned, implemented and evaluated to meet the children's aptitudes and needs'.

4. (*Mr Houlden*) 'Teacher appraisal is to assess how far schools and their departments have met their objectives in relation to improving pupil performance. It is about the quality of the educational process'.

This emphasis on process comes through strongly in all the papers. Evaluation and assessment, in all their aspects, are seen as essential factors in improving the general functioning of the school, promoting the efficiency and professional development of teachers, and assisting and motivating the pupils to greater achievement. And quality is to be judged, not solely by end results, useful though these are for particular purposes, but also by the nature and manner of the learning that takes place, and the human relationships that support it.

Seen in that light, evaluation is both a means to improving the educational process and part of it. To quote *Mr Price*...'...evaluation of the progress made is more than a procedure in the network of activity. It is a process, even an attitude, which operates throughout the cycle of planning, resourcing, teaching, development and assessment and tends to constant self and corporate evaluation...; an awareness and acceptance that we are all professionally accountable to ourselves, each other and our pupils'.

It is a form of accountability which puts assessment and appraisal in their correct and acceptable professional context. In recent years, as national economies grew shakier and money tighter, there has been much demand, not only in this country, for greater accountability in education: and given the size of the bill, a reasonable request. Often, though, it has been argued in the cost-effective terms of manufacturing industry, with the pupils regarded as products off the school assembly line, and their assessed achievements as indices of how far public money has been properly spent. Happily, there have not lacked percipient writers to point out the naivete and inappropriateness of this model. It is inappropriate because, unlike a manufacturing industry, which seeks to provide, at minimum cost, a standard product conforming to exact specification with as little variation as possible, the school is seeking, within the time and resources available, to develop individual human beings as fully as possible. The more successfully it does so, the more divergent, beyond certain basic competencies, the pupils are likely to become.

It is not a matter of shaping inert raw material but an interactive process between the minds and personalities of teachers and pupils, the outcomes of which can never be wholly foreseen. True education is, in a desirable sense, ungovernable, and the results unpredictable. Which is why many schools and individual pupils succeed beyond expectation, despite the odds.

In any case, much that may be valuably taught and learned in schools is not amenable to measurement, not only because the instruments may be lacking but also because the outcomes may not be apparent till much later, if at all. It may be totally impossible to establish simple patterns of cause and effect.

None of which detracts from the importance of those assessments which can properly be made, nor absolves teachers and schools from any accountability. It does shift the emphasis from exclusive preoccupation with the results of learning, which are only partly assessable, to concern for the process and the quality of opportunities created.

Such accountability must rest primarily on principles of professional practice and responsibility towards the young. It must also include readiness to communicate and explain what the school is attempting to do, and why. School governors, the LEA, parents and a much wider general public all have a stake, and a right to know. A requirement of explanation is not an infringement of professional rights, but a recognition that professional judgements may need interpretation, at a variety of levels. Schools no less than governments need to get their presentation right. For the teachers, in day-to-day terms, it means the conscientious exercise of a complex of skills, well described in a quotation for which I am indebted to the Suffolk study of teacher appraisal: 'Effective teaching is not simply a matter of implementing a small number of basic teaching skills. Instead, effective teaching requires the ability to implement a very large number of diagnostic, instructional, managerial and therapeutic skills, tailoring behaviour in specific contexts and situations to the needs of the moment. Effective teachers not only must be able to do a large number of things; they must also be able to recognise which of the many things they know how to do applies at a given moment and be able to follow through by performing the behaviour effectively.' Such inspired opportunism has also to be related to longer-term goals, and has to take constant account of what *Mr Price*, in his paper, has called 'The condition of the pupils'.

Schools exercise a considerable professional freedom within a 'given' framework which both enables and limits. The size of the school, whether it is single-sexed or mixed, the staffing ratio and the training system which produced the teachers, the buildings and material resources, the capitation allowance, all rest on policies determined outside the school. Such policies may change, or can be changed — for example, the levels of expenditure or the nature of the teacher-training system — and the schools themselves may provide part of the evidence for the need for change. There are other factors which are not within control of the education system, but which profoundly affect educational achievement: the nature of the environment in which the school is situated, the health of the pupils and their families, the social conditions in which they live, the educational experience and expectations of the parents, the local mixture of racial and linguistic origins and religious beliefs, economic prospects and employment opportunities — all these, as well as the individual characteristics of the pupils themselves, affect the response of the pupils, and their capacity to respond, to what the schools have to offer. *Mr Houlden* reminds us 'Pupils are not all of equal ability, parental support is not universal, and individuals grow and develop at different rates'; and *Mr Price* observes 'More children fail in school due to a lack of personal security and a state of unhappiness than lack of ability... When the pupil is assessed then the contributions of all influences are assessed and the pupil's achievements are not a single measure of the teacher's efficiency'. Nevertheless, when a school seeks to assure itself, and to be able to demonstrate to others, that it is doing the best that it can for the pupils in its care, the touchstone must be the progressive achievement of the pupils. That, in turn, implies the need for agreed principles and consistent policies for assessment, and a framework of practice to which all teachers, whatever their special subjects or areas of interest, can relate.

Mrs Spaull's paper shows the staff of a primary school recognising their need for improved knowledge of the purposes and techniques of assessment and seeking to extend their studies in the evaluation of children's work and progress. The attempt has led also to systematic study of each part of the curriculum, and to improved observation and recording.

The two secondary school papers point up the still greater complexity of the task in a large secondary school. *Mr Price's* paper illustrates in detail one school's policies in action, covering a range of monitoring and testing appropriate to a wide curriculum, records of attainment and progress embodying teachers' assessments, and records of achievement, going well beyond work in the classroom, to which the pupils themselves contribute. An explanatory booklet setting out principles and practice is available not only to staff but, notably to parents, and helps to make sense of what can otherwise be the bemusing shorthand of school reports. *Mr Houlden's* paper similarly emphasises the need for a positive framework as part of a whole school policy which includes routine marking, graded assessments, a graduated profile of achievement and a record of individuals' developing interests and pursuits. In each case there is a supporting organisational network of staff with co-ordinating and tutorial responsibilities. Both papers stress the importance, whilst also acknowledging the difficulty, of assessing personal qualities and achievements, as well as academic attainments, and recognising the need to bring both pupils and their parents into consultation.

All the activities thus described are school-initiated and are part of the larger process of self-evaluation. For secondary schools, there is, however, the additional evidence of performance in public examinations, which give some comparative reference beyond the individual school. We all know the pitfalls of comparative league tables, and of excessive veneration for what in the end are fairly crude, summary judgements. But for the individual school and its pupils and their parents, successful performance in external examinations is a reassurance (what it does for the unsuccessful is another matter). 16-plus examinations, in particular, have long been an influence in setting standards; they have also powerfully affected what is taught and the manner of the teaching in secondary schools. Impending changes could make them a more positive influence for good. The current rethinking of syllabus content and objectives, the inclusion of more oral and course work, and the eventual shift, if indeed it can be managed, to criterion-referenced assessment, could have a beneficial backwash on the work of schools, not only in the examination classes. It may well be that even as we reform 16-plus exams, mass examining at that stage is already obsolescent, or will soon be rendered so by other factors. As the tendency increases, for economic as much as educational reasons, for most of the 16–19 population to remain in some form of continuing education or training, assessment of what the students can do and have become by 17, 18 or 19 will be of more direct relevance to their subsequent employment or acceptance into higher education. By the time the fully reformed GCSE is in place, other developments may well have overtaken it. But the demise of 16-plus is not yet: alternative structures pre-and post-16 are not yet adequately articulated or secured by experience, and if assessment at that stage is ultimately to become largely or wholly internal to the schools, most teachers will need improved skills and knowledge and some external framework of guidance and support. Meanwhile, current developments could provide the occasion of valuable training opportunities, and schools might go further and profitably explore ways of assessing group projects and inter-disciplinary work which are difficult in any case to encompass in external subject-based examinations. Given, too, the importance attached to work experience and community service in many programmes, some ways of assessing the nature of the experience and the quality of the participation seem desirable. So pray for virtue, but not yet, and meanwhile make the most of what can be learned from examination reforms in progress.

However it goes, there is a substantial workload ahead for teachers. Primary schools escape the particular pressure of public examinations, though not those for improved and progressive assessment in many areas of learning; both primary teachers and secondary teachers alike are also caught up in substantial curricular changes — for example, in the introduction of science or in the extensive rethinking of the content and manner of its teaching.

Staff-appraisal can properly take its place in such a context, as a means of helping teachers the better to equip themselves for the job, and as a way of encouraging them to find new opportunities for personal and professional satisfaction.

The four papers we have all express concern to promote the professional development of teachers in both their pedagogic and management skills, and to identify in-service training needs. All emphasise that a climate of mutual confidence is necessary, and the need for appraisal to be seen as a positive and corporate activity. *Mrs Spaull* comments 'Evaluation and appraisal exercises will flourish in any school where the ethos and climate are right — where there is sensitive leadership and full staff consultation'.

That climate, as *Mrs Spaull's* paper also illustrates, may be partly the outcome of attitudes and habits of working built up long before any formal scheme is embarked upon.

Mr Taylor's account interestingly illustrates how experience gained by head and staff in developing role descriptions and job definitions makes formal appraisal more readily acceptable, as an extension of known practice rather than complete innovation.

Mr Houlden declares 'Any school can start on developing its assessment policies providing the preconditions for change exist. These include an open-management style and an outward-looking philosophy which will help neutralise the threats assumed to be implicit in the concept of appraisal'.

Those 'threats' will diminish if appraisal is seen as enabling good teachers to extend their range and find new stimulus, and not only as a means of identifying lame ducks or rescuing teachers in difficulty.

Mr Price sets out, in more detail than can fairly be represented by a brief quotation, strategies for creating a suitable environment in which professional awareness and acceptance of responsibility are fostered, and 'agreed principles are supported by effective structures, organisation and management'. Again, 'open management' is stressed, and the importance of 'a structure of communication, consultation and participation'.

Of the many messages to be taken up from these papers, I would especially note the evolutionary aspect. A school needs to be at a stage of professional readiness to embark on any substantial programme of staff-appraisal or self-evaluation. To that extent, schemes originating from a school's own initiative seem likelier to succeed than exercises arbitrarily imposed from outside.

Which does not mean, of course, that an LEA anxious to embark on a programme of systematic evaluation with its schools must hold off forever or until each school signals that it is sitting comfortably. It does suggest that LEA-initiated schemes may best begin with good pilot runs in those schools, possibly only a small minority, which already by their style of working have established the necessary preconditions, or feel themselves to have done so.

While the volunteers pioneer the schemes, and help to refine them, other schools could, and should, be helped to develop the necessary strengths in communication, consultation and management, and, especially where assessment of teachers is involved, in observation and interviewing. Effective job-description, as an essential basis, as well as a useful staging post towards staff-appraisal, might be part of the preparation. Helping schools to help themselves implies supportive intervention, the main weight of which must fall on LEA advisory and inspectorate services, although other agencies may be called in aid.

The four school papers confirm the value of outside help in the conduct of appraisal, whether of teachers or of classroom work, in the form of consultants, or 'critical friends'. Such help may come from colleges or universities or from other heads and experienced teachers, as well as from LEA advisers. These are important resources, valuable in giving the school points of reference outside itself. But multiplied up into a general plan for a whole LEA area or, indeed, all LEA areas, the implications for professional manpower are formidable and suggest a need for co-ordination, though with enough flexibility to enable schools to capitalise on personal contacts already established.

Mrs Spaull usefully stresses the importance of making clear what is required of the consultants, in order that they may make an effective contribution.

The papers touch on the practicability of involving staff in appraisal of the head, and give one or two indications of how, in the right climate, staff can be given the opportunity to say honestly how well they perceive the head to be doing his job, at least in relation to themselves and their areas of work. As part of 'open' management this is valuable and could be the starting point of some self-appraisal by the head. But something more, which must include an overview from outside, is also needed if heads are to be fully and fairly assessed. This again implies provision made through, but not necessarily exclusively by, the LEA. It must, once more, fall heavily on LEA advisers and inspectors, but could also operate through area panels of recently retired or seconded heads. (The Suffolk report[1] discusses some interesting possibilities.)

---

[1] See paper 4.1.

In all of this, what about school governors and parents? Most governors derive virtually all their knowledge of the school from reports presented by the head, plus occasional attendance at special functions. Those reports commonly offer a succinct, factual account of things done — examination results, sports activities, new staff appointments, plus details of coming events and some highlighting of current needs: all appropriate and useful enough, but relatively inert information, apart from those items which carry a financial kick. Less commonly, but more stimulatingly, routine reports may also set current concerns in a context of plans and hopes for the future; they may float ideas for discussion and positively invite comment on policies and problems. Many governors anxious to make a real contribution would welcome such invitations, but in order to make a proper response, they need first a closer acquaintance with the working life of the school. Without encroaching on the professional responsibilites of the head and staff, the governors also have responsibilites towards the school: they must be able to ask searching questions and to appreciate the significance of the answers. They cannot do this if their knowledge is confined to relatively short meetings three or four times a year, and the occasional social function.

It might be good policy to invite governors individually to associate themselves with particular aspects of the school's life, in and out of the classroom, and for the head to ensure that there are opportunities to get to know the members of staff most involved, and to sit in on staff meetings from time to time, when relevant matters are under discussion. The head, in turn, when he comes to give his reports to the governing body, could count on at least a nucleus of well-informed and attentive listeners, who would be better placed, in light of their first-hand knowledge, to support projected development and requests for resources.

Some governors might well be recruited to the network of 'critical friends' needed by the school — not, normally, to take part as assessors in formal appraisal, but to raise questions and sometimes, as interested outsiders, to help staff put familiar problems into new perspectives. Governors often include local employers and people from a variety of working backgrounds, as well as teachers and parents. Together, they could convey some of the concerns and expectations of the local community.

Associating parents, other than those who happen also to be governors, is much more difficult, if only because the number of people to be contacted is so much larger and not all can, or will, respond. But most parents feel themselves to have a stake in the school as far as the well-being of their own children is concerned, and through the children they have some perception, however partial, of how well the school functions. They need opportunity to make known these impressions, and, if necessary, help in formulating them. *Mrs*

Spaull's paper illustrates, for example, a modest but interesting attempt, evidently welcomed, to sound out parents' views on priorities for evaluation. Schools do, increasingly, make efforts to inform and explain to parents; they need also to listen and to respond. But to do that well, like so much else that is desirable, takes time.

In almost all the developments being discussed here there are implications for additional time and manpower, in both schools and LEA services. There may be some savings at the margins of existing resources that could still be made, by modifying present practices and improving organisation and communication: and sometimes improvements in the use of staff, though not savings in cost, could be made by releasing teachers from tasks more appropriately done by clerical and technical assistants. But there is little reason to suppose that there is much slack in either school staffs or LEA services, and much of what is being advocated involves sensitive handling of human beings, where time for consultation, observation, reflection and discussion is essential.

There are many implications for preparatory training, if appraisal and evaluation are to find a proper place in all schools: there are criteria to be developed, and skills to be acquired or improved in different forms of assessment, in observation and recording, and in the interpretation of data. There are other implications for in-service training in light of the outcomes of evaluation, as part of both staff development and curriculum renewal. Much of the effort will run to waste unless results can be followed up and experience shared through local or national courses and professional publications.

Some further work on costing and logistics, undertaken by LEAs jointly with their schools, would help make planning as realistic as possible.

The need for a continuing programme of staff-appraisal and development, and for improved modes of assessing and recording the achievements of pupils, would have to be set alongside other intermittent needs for evaluation of a school as a whole or of selected aspects of its work, with room still to deal also with unforeseen contingencies. (A report such as that of Professor Egglestone's study[1] of the educational experience of 15–18 year olds from minority ethnic groups might well get a school, or an LEA on behalf of its schools, urgently reviewing assumptions and practices.)

Clearly, there has to be some selection of priorities, and recognition that these may vary with local circumstances or the stage of development of particular schools. A school's perception of its own needs has to be taken into account by an authority developing policies

---

[1] *The Educational and Vocational Experience of 15-18 Year Old Young People of Ethnic Minority Groups.* Multicultural Studies in Higher Education, University of Warwick, October 1985.

for a whole local area, just as central government's policies must allow for the distinctive circumstances of particular authorities.

Time and manpower apart, there are human limits in any case to the number of substantial exercises and inquiries any institution can sustain simultaneously, in addition to meeting the regular demands of the job. There must be a moral somewhere in *Mrs Spaull's* moving story of how, when her staff were busy with working parties and data-gathering for several major reviews at once, they were brought to a standstill 'when extensive dry rot was found in the school...' There's a lot of it about: too few busy people chasing too many papers or filling in endless questionnaires, and dry rot is never far away. There is always a danger in over-ambitious, global exercises that information gathering becomes an end in itself, and not enough time is left over for putting the information to use. Selectivity is not only a matter of working realistically within available resources, but also of pacing, and of allowing for the complexity and sensitivity of the tasks. These decisions cannot all be taken by the schools alone, though neither can they be taken without them. Without the schools' willing commitment, schemes imposed wholly from outside have little chance of success. Schools have the star role, but they also need support, advice and resources.

To promote nationally improved assessment of the pupils, constructive school evaluation and curriculum development, and a system of appraising teachers that is effective and fair requires:

— An efficient programme of training, flexible enough to respond to changing needs.

— Points of reference and critical professional advice outside the schools themselves.

— Guidelines relating to curricular aims and criteria for assessment and appraisal negotiated and agreed locally.

— Adequate material resources and appropriate working conditions.

— Recognition of the demands on time, particularly of teachers and of LEA services, realistically costed in a programme of development for an area.

— Acceptance by the schools that capacity to benefit from support implies an openness to outside views, and responsiveness, particularly to parents and the local community.

I end with some words from *Mr Houlden's* paper, in which he reflects on the purpose of all this activity:

'The principles upon which the appraisal of the pupils and teachers are based are very much the same. The need is for positive evaluation to be used alongside criteria-related academic assessments for pupils, because it is attitude, commitment and values, as well as academic performance, which are important to society at large. For teachers, too, a positive framework for appraisal is essential because it provides the key to staff development and the improvement of the service. For in all schools, assessment should be an open exercise and one which is integral to the educational process. They should know what is going on and be invited to contribute to it. Learning is a process, not a product. In the final analysis appraisal is about the quality of that process. The principle to bear in mind is that we should educate people for what they might have the capacity to become, and so not be content with objectives which are solely instrumental.'

PRESENTATION 3

The Role and Responsibility of the School

3.1 Watergall Junior School, Peterborough

Fred Taylor, formerly Headteacher

This paper describes the aims, methods of introduction, procedures employed and the outcome of a teacher appraisal strategy in use at Watergall Junior School at the time of writing. The school has a head, deputy head, seven Scale 2 teachers and three Scale 1 teachers. It is a Group 5 junior school with 330 children on roll. The building, of semi-open plan design, was opened in 1976 to serve a community within a Development Corporation estate in Greater Peterborough. The children are taught in parallel mixed ability classes in each year group. The Scale 2 teachers are each responsible for an area of the curriculum, eg. environmental studies or mathematics, working to job descriptions (Appendix 1) which have been agreed between themselves, the head and governors. Their roles involve the evaluation of children's work throughout the school across the curriculum area for which they are responsible. The instrument described here was designed to appraise these postholders in order to extend and improve their performance in management and teaching skills. Such a system can be adapted to appraise classroom teaching performance in a similar way.

Aims and objectives

The appraisal system is designed to fulfill the following aim:

    a. to ensure that each area of the curriculum is successfully planned, implemented and evaluated to meet the children's aptitudes and needs.

This main aim is underpinned by objectives which:

    a. assess the strengths and weaknesses of postholders;

    b. identify areas of teaching and learning where development is needed;

    c. encourage feedback for teachers on their performance;

    d. clarify the functions of the postholders to an extent that reduces ambiguity and role conflict.

In order to meet the aim the appraisal system has been developed in ways that:

a. encourage a commitment to appraisal by giving the postholders an opportunity to be fully involved in all decision-making, planning and implementation of the system;

b. meets the particular needs of the school by appropriately maintaining each curriculum area.

Method of introducing and designing the system

It was necessary to establish the climate and the agreed need for an appraisal system within the school. Aims and consequent implications for individual teachers within the school were discussed in order to allay the initial anxiety of teachers and dispel the notion that they would be expected to fulfil all the requirements in any list of functions from the outset. The procedure for defining the roles of postholders was well established and the appraisal system was therefore an extension of practice rather than a complete innovation. Following initial discussions Scale 2 teachers were invited individually to set out the most important functions of their role. These separate lists were amalgamated by the head and checked by the teachers to ensure that none of their original comments had been omitted. The composite list (Appendix 2) was then ordered by a group of headteachers and with slight changes accepted by the postholders.

The teachers were then invited to list the sub-functions which underpinned the three main functions, items 1–3. In time this practice will be extended to include all functions on the list. The separate lists of sub-functions (Appendix 3) were then amalgamated by the head and agreed in a similar manner. This method affords all participants the opportunity to contribute and in this way enhances individual feelings of commitment to the appraisal instrument. It also ensures that the instrument contains functions of the postholder's role recognised as important by all teachers in the school, although differing contributions and weighting of importance also depend on experience in post and consequent knowledge of the school and its community. Although the original decision to introduce the appraisal system was taken by the head in an attempt to clarify and improve existing practice, it had the full agreement of the staff. It can consequently be recognised as an organic model of institutional development rooted in teacher contribution and participation rather than a management directive.

The appraisal system in practice

Teachers within the scheme are invited to an appraisal meeting with the headteacher after completing the relevant sections of the form (Appendix 4). Responses to this form show the perception which they have of their success in carrying-out the functions contained in the instrument. The headteacher also completes a copy of the form from his viewpoint. At the subsequent meeting agreement is reached as to the precise nature of the development which is required to improve the pupils' performance in the curriculum area being considered. After this meeting has taken place a critical friend/neighbouring headteacher visits the school and using the completed forms as a reference triangulates the validity of the agreements in discussion with various teachers and by observing teaching practice and the children at work. After his report has been received performance objectives are agreed between the headteacher and individual postholders forming the practical targets of growth change and development for a specified period of time. This development may be concerned with schemes of work, teaching methods or the performance of pupils within specific age groups or ability ranges. In one case the art and craft postholder agreed that a series of finished pieces of work should be evaluated to determine the success of particular teaching and learning strategies and also to develop teachers own analytical expertise. Whilst such performance objectives are being considered the headteacher is responsible for the provision of help and guidance and the involvement of LEA officers who are able to assist towards a successful outcome.

This may involve in-service courses, suggested reading material, visits to other schools or expert advice. Clearly teachers new to their posts are concerned to achieve performance objectives which will establish their credibility within the school as curriculum consultants (see Appendix 3, Section 1). However, all postholders work through the appraisal instrument developing their managerial and teaching competence as they proceed. Whilst this description discusses the positive growth and development of individual postholders, it can be seen that such a system is also designed to highlight general school weaknesses requiring remedial action by the head teacher and governor of the school. For example, a teacher unable to proceed through Appendix 3, Section 1 and become credible by demonstrating good practice would need to spend time observing and teaching alongside an established colleague. Such an arrangement would require sensitive handling by the head teacher and may necessitate financial assistance for supply cover.

After the specified period of time, agreed in the performance objective which varies according to the circumstance and the task, the second appraisal meeting takes place and this includes reference to the report of the critical friend who has visited the school again to note the development.

Issues arising from the system

The problems involved in the implementation of the strategy are concerned mainly with the time required to carry out the procedures thoroughly, staff turnover, commitment and the extent to which objectivity and rigour can be assured. The headteacher's time taken up in meetings which may last for one or two hours for each postholder and may be required twice termly is difficult to find at the already busy start and finish of each term. Experience has shown that the critical friend required two full days twice each term for his observations to be worthwhile.

A significant decline in the rate of improvement can come as a result of staff turnover since incoming members feel less commitment to the system. This can be reduced by the careful explanation of the school's management strategies at the pre-application stage of an appointment procedure and by job descriptions which set out the evaluation strategies employed.

All teachers and schools are the subject of continual evaluation, assessment and appraisal, conducted by members of the school and the community, however informed, misguided or poorly rooted in fact this may be. If such appraisal is practised in the way described in this paper teachers and schools can feel secure in the knowledge that assessment is being carried out in an objective, informed and open manner, and members of the community can be reassured by the governors that development-based appraisal is taking place.

This important outcome of enhanced professionalism is recognised as extremely beneficial by the teachers being appraised, as they are aware that skills and competencies being acquired could aid their promotion to senior posts in other schools. The problems of over-critical teachers and dissent from findings are minimised when a system employs agreed performance objectives. Such matters can be dealt with by the head in appraisal meetings and during the implementation, enabling the teachers to proceed with the knowledge that they have approval for their actions. The headteacher must recognise that improved effectiveness only comes when objectives have a likelihood of success and match accordingly when the agreement is being reached.

Outcomes

The headteacher and postholders are primarily concerned with improving pupil performance. After teachers' and pupils' work has been evaluated and weaknesses recognised it is possible to decide on pertinent action by the postholders. For example, a recent objective of the science postholder was to:

assist colleagues in planning work which focused on:

a. problem-solving activities and opportunities for all children;

b. observation and accurate recording for older pupils;

c. the development of a questioning attitude in the younger pupils.

After the implementation of this objective the critical friend reported that:

a. colleagues have found the science workshops useful;

b. the postholder has perceived colleagues' needs and made arrangements to work alongside them;

c. the postholder is very aware of the need to bring people forward from where they are;

d. problem-solving was in evidence and talking to children about their work revealed a high level of success in all but one of the classes;

e. the children had devised tests for the material they were using and experimented to find the best way of doing things;

Poor implementation by the class teacher of realistic objectives planned by the postholders often stems from an individual's inability to organise teaching and learning activities in a completely successful way. A further stage in the school's development would be to employ the methods described above in order to design an instrument relating to the role of a class teacher.

Conclusion

The aim of this system is to improve pupil performance by involving postholders in a series of management activities which enable them to plan, implement and evaluate the teaching and learning within the school across a curriculum area. It enables teachers to consider objectively their professional development and involves the head in an evaluation of performance leading to coherent judgements about development needs. Most importantly it affords teachers the opportunity to be involved in planning their own development based on their perceived needs. The claim is that teachers are more likely to work towards the aims of development based appraisal and consequent school improvement if they are given the responsibility of full participation.

APPENDIX 1

Job description — mathematics Scale 2

1. Aims:

i. to oversee mathematics in school;

ii. to assist in general discipline;

iii. to set a high standard with own class which can be used as a guide to levels of expectation in mathematics.

2. *General organisation:*

    i. to order and take responsibility for mathematics equipment and ensure that each class is equipped;

    ii. to co-ordinate a display of mathematics work in the school;

    iii. to call in children's books at regular intervals with a view to checking:

        a. the match or work being undertaken;

        b. the continuity from year to year;

        c. method of marking and recording progress;

        d. presentation and general standard of children's work.

    iv. to assist and support new members of staff with the understanding of school policy.

3. *Curriculum responsibility:*

    i. to be responsible for liaison with other stages and to report to the governors when required;

    ii. to lead staff meeting when necessary to further develop mathematics in the school;

    iii. to heighten interest and enthusiasm in the subject.

    iv. to keep the school aware of developments in all aspects of the subject;

    v. to be responsible for liaison with other postholders to ensure that mathematics is integrated within the curriculum.

APPENDIX 2

List of functions drawn up by individual postholders and co-ordinated by the head

1. To set a high standard in own class which can be used as a guide to expectation and a model of good practice.

2. To provide help and guidance for all colleagues (whether new to the school or not) in planning their children's work.

3. To lead staff meetings and discuss the area of responsibility in order to facilitate a good understanding and utilisation of school policy through guidelines.

4. To evaluate the children's work and report to head before discussing findings with colleagues.

5. To co-ordinate displays in the school which promote and enhance the curriculum activity for which responsibility has been given.

6. To keep the school informed of developments which may affect its performance.

7. To ensure the sensible allocation of finance in order to provide and maintain a wide variety of materials and apparatus for all ability groups.

8. To report to the head and governors as and when required to keep them fully informed of all activities related to the area of specific responsibility.

9. To liaise with other educational phases in the community in conjunction with other feeder schools.

10. To run extra curricula clubs in own subject in order to extend teaching and interest beyond own class.

APPENDIX 3

The list of sub-functions which forms the appraisal instrument

1. To set high standards in own class which can be used as a guide to expectation and a model of good practice.

   a. *Organisation should show evidence of*:
      i. good classroom organisation and appropriate arrangements of space, resources and time;
      ii. curriculum planning and teaching which takes account of a wide range of ability, match, teacher expectation, relationships/atmosphere recording and evaluation;
      iii. creativity and enthusiasm for own curriculum area;
      iv. obvious strength in own specialist area but also general all-round ability as a class teacher;
      v. own practice resulting in making and/or testing of teaching materials to form a resource bank;
      vi. the demonstration of good policy in action;
      vii. sound discipline underpinned by good organisation and good relationships;
      viii. the demonstration of a well balanced curriculum.

   b. *Display should be*:
      i. pertinent to work in hand and up-to-date;
      ii. arranged to include material which shows a variety of activities and skills and a good cross-section of ability within the class;
      iii. It should:
         — enhance the children's sense of achievement
         — promote an attitude which pursues high standards
         — provide a stimulating environment
         — have clear relevance to own specialism

2. To provide help and guidance for all colleagues (whether new to the school or not) in planning their children's work.
   i. provide clear guidelines;
   ii. demonstrate an ability to form effective professional relationships with colleagues;
   iii. provide resources which are adequate to meet the needs of all teachers;
   iv. positively help and encourage all staff during teaching sessions;

105

    v. have a good personal understanding of specialist area across the span of primary education;

  vi. be available for discussion in non-teaching time;

 vii. understand from observation and evaluation the strengths and weaknesses of colleagues and give appropriate support;

viii. to keep adequate records of completed work in order to ensure the continuity and co-ordination of teaching throughout the school.

  ix. develop individual skills in colleagues;

   x. encourage teachers to utilise their previous experience and participate fully in evaluation in order to strengthen the policy through the continual revitalisation and renewal of guidelines;

  xi. to strive to become more competent in all curriculum areas;

 xii. to manage meetings sensitively and efficiently;

xiii. be consistent with advice. Firm but working from the supportive stance of 'How can I help you to do your job better?'

xiv. return to staff to remind them as often as necessary of what is required;

 xv. understand the relationship with colleague specialists and help staff to integrate teaching when desirable;

xvi. be aware of individuals' understanding and commitment to the policy.

3. To lead staff meetings and discuss the area of responsibility in order to facilitate a good understanding and utilisation of school policy through guidelines.

    i. to involve fully all staff in the preparation of guidelines and direct the school's activity in own curriculum area;

   ii. arrange for a feeling of ownership built up in a climate of objective-centred problem-solving activity;

  iii. be able to explain the school's approach and its theoretical background to teaching;

  iv. organise and run workshops and meetings in order to deepen the understanding and be willing to discuss openly and be questioned;

   v. illustrate discussion with examples from within the school;

  vi. be prepared to lead and take responsibility in a positive way;

 vii. encourage colleagues to feel that they are part of a team;

viii. provide an opportunity for every teacher to contribute to the evaluation process and modify the guidelines in the light of experience;

  ix. arrange for discussion between specialist, head and individual teacher after an evaluation of particular pieces of work has taken place;

   x. demonstrate continuity and its advantages by using examples of the children's work;

  xi. be understanding about the difficulties of non-specialists;

 xii. organise a resource base and inform staff of use and availability;

xiii. organise visits to schools which demonstrate good practice;

xiv. circulate papers which will inform colleagues of recent developments in own specialist area;

xv. encourage a responsibility for the curriculum area by all staff — not merely the PSR holder;

xvi. demonstrate a consistency in following the agreed policy;

xvii. be confident but accept criticism — accept that the children are more important than ones own ego;

xviii. encourage creativity/flair/individuality in the choice of a stimulating content through which the skills, attitudes and concepts agreed in the guidelines can be taught in a way that enhances the children's experience.

APPENDIX 4

TEACHER APPRAISAL FORM: WATERGALL JUNIOR SCHOOL

MAIN FUNCTION: to set high standards in own class which can be used as a guide to expectation and a model of good practice.

SUB-FUNCTIONS (see list)

		Teacher's Comments	Head's Comments	Agreed Objectives
a.	i.			
	ii.			
	iii.			
	iv.			
	v.			
	vi.			
	vii.			
	viii.			
b.	i.			
	ii.			
	iii.			

Acknowledgements

The success of this work has been made possible by the excellent co-operation of colleagues at Watergall both past and present. We are also indebted to Cambridgeshire LEA and the staff of the education management department at North-East London Polytechnic for the support which the school has received.

The Role and Responsibility of the School

3.2 Morley Victoria Junior and Infants School, Leeds

Sylvia M Spaull, Headteacher

Aims

The aims of evaluation and assessment are to improve pupil performance and understanding and enhance the quality of the teaching and learning process.

The objectives are:

1. To encourage active co-operation among staff leading to personal and professional development.

2. To improve teacher morale and increase professionalism.

3. To provide new perspectives and challenges for teachers.

4. To improve curricular, organisational and managerial skills in the school.

5. To assess the school's needs and priorities for development.

6. To meet the professional development needs of teachers alongside the needs of the school.

Procedures employed

The evaluation procedures employed at Morley Victoria School have been developed over a number of years since the appointment of the present headteacher in January 1976. The school was then Group 3 with 90 children on roll, aged 5–7. These children occupied approximately a third of a large stone building, with first- and second-year children from the local high school occupying the other part, plus 11 outer classroom units on the campus. The main school building is a fine example of the best modern architecture of the late 19th century and was built as a progressive board school in 1901. It stands north of the town of Morley, a distributive centre (population 44,122) four miles from the city of Leeds. In July 1976 the high school children left these premises and went into new buildings, and in the September of that year the infant school, established for 75 years, began to expand into the present Group 6 infant, junior and nursery school with 420 children on roll.

The years of growth meant the appointment of many new members of staff and together we worked to create the present school. Every aspect of school life had to be studied; aims, policies, and priorities discussed, formulated and recorded; schemes and guidelines produced. An important part of our studies in the early years of growth was how best to devise systems for assessment and recording of children's learning, and work by the National Federation for Educational Research (NFER) and the Assessment of Performance Unit (APU) was studied along with advice from advisers and educational psychologists.

These activities necessitated regular staff consultation; group problem solving; the setting up of objectives and targets; the sharing of expertise; and the establishment of good working relationships. Every aspect of school life had to be studied in a short space of time; therefore some of the studies were inevitably rather superficial and the invitation received in the spring of 1982, to take part in a Schools Council self-evaluation project called 'Guidelines for Review and Internal Development in Schools' (GRIDS) was very timely.*

GRIDS is a systematic approach to self-evaluation of policy and practice in a school. It makes explicit that which has always been implicit in a good school. Its strength lies in the initial stages when staff are encouraged to analyse present practice before following a systematic process which facilitates the transition from the review stage to the development and evaluation stages. It has logical simplicity but it first requires a school to examine the need and desire for such an exercise. Its success largely depends on the existing climate and ethos of the school where there must be mutual trust between head and teachers, committed staff, good communications, cohesion and sensitive leadership.

Methods of introduction

The evaluation methods used at the school have stemmed from initial commonsense evaluation to the systematic GRIDS approach. The initial presentation of this self-evaluation programme was made to all staff in March 1982: previous discussion with the deputy head had identified the need and desire to be a part of the project — our school was ready — the climate was right. The majority of staff agreed; they thought it would be a challenge to take part, a chance to review the school as a team and re-think development and progress to date. One member of staff had reservations about its value to the school and

---

* The GRIDS project stemmed from a conference organised by the Schools Council at Stoke Rochford in February 1981. There, good practices on whole school self-evaluation known to exist in a number of LEAs, plus work in other countries (eg. early work done by Per Dalin in Norway) were studied. The council commissioned a team of four, based at Bristol University, to produce the guideline materials, which in 1982 were tested in 31 primary and secondary schools in five LEAs. In spring 1984 two handbooks describing the GRIDS process were published by Longmans (see also paper 4.2.)

requested not to play a key part in the project but to co-operate with others if the work seemed relevant to the need of the school.

The GRIDS programme has five clearly defined stages which we followed closely:

STAGE 1. GETTING STARTED: At the first meeting clarification of why we wanted to undertake a school self-review and the implications of using the GRIDS process were discussed. The deputy head ensured that every member of staff was aware of the school's existing policies on all aspects of school life.

STAGE 2. INITIAL REVIEW: An anonymously completed questionnaire was used to allow staff to express their views cf the school's strengths and weaknesses. The questionnaire listed aspects of school life under three headings: curriculum; pupils; staff and organisation; and asked to say what aspects of the school should have priority for a specific review (Appendix 1).

Collated survey results created lively discussions as joint criteria and priorities for review were chosen.

STAGE 3. SPECIFIC REVIEW(S): Originally the school chose to undertake three specific review studies highlighted from the survey results, these were: 'Work in science'; 'Procedures for testing and assessment'; and 'Work in PE'. Specific review teams were chosen, comprising three or four teachers for each topic, led by a team co-ordinator. The task of each team was to collect and analyse evidence of the strengths and weaknesses of present practices and then make recommendations for changes which, if agreed by the staff as a whole, would then be put into action. Unfortunately at this stage of our involvement with the project extensive dry rot was found in the school and we had to vacate the main school building for the school year 1982–83 whilst work to cure the rot was carried out. This necessitated the infants working in outside classrooms and the juniors being transported daily to a school two miles away. Due to the problems of the split school it was decided that only one review would be undertaken initially and the staff chose 'Work in science'. In hindsight the commitment required by the team and the time involved, for meetings, study and visits both in and out of school, plus the importance of involving all the staff at every stage, lead me to suggest that primary schools undertake only one review study of this kind at the start. Our second review on 'Testing and assessment procedures' began in February 1983, and our third review on 'PE' began in January 1985. (Review teams met formerly once a week, sometimes in school time but more often at lunch-times or after school. They regularly reported back to all the staff at the general staff meetings held once a fortnight. They did their own research and only requested help of the headteacher when advice, visits, or consultants were needed — or extra resources of time and money!)

STAGE 4. ACTION FOR DEVELOPMENT: The recommendations for change and development produced by the review teams included devising new schemes of work in two of our three reviews ('Science' and 'PE'). During this development stage it was felt that staff would benefit from in-service training, and we began to work closely with outside consultants from the LEA and local colleges and universities. All three of the specific reviews have involved outside consultants. For science we were encouraged to involve two college lecturers from a LEA college of education. In retrospect it was not a total success: meetings were rather contrived, mainly instigated to satisfy the trial of the process we were following and the school did not make explicit what role was required of the consultants. Having learned from early mistakes, consultants used in our studies on testing and assessment procedures and work in PE were called in when the team felt there was a need. We tried to define clearly what was wanted and expected from these consultants: help and advice to enable us to find the right answers, but it was made clear that the school would make its own decisions. The consultants were asked to give us new perspectives, to raise questions we had not considered, and ensure that the self-evaluation study was not just a pooling of ignorance or a reinforcement of mediocrity. The evaluation work undertaken at this stage showed that there was an improvement in the quality of what was being taught and enables us to extend this in further study of what we should teach, how we should teach, how pupils learn and how we can best match our teaching to individual pupils' abilities and aptitudes.

STAGE 5. OVERVIEW AND RE-START: We are currently involved in this stage of GRIDS with comparisons being made between how things were and how they now stand. We have recently re-started the GRIDS cycle. Teachers who were on the staff in March 1982 have completed their second survey and those who have joined us since have been introduced to the process. This time we have extended the involvement to governors and parents.

GOVERNORS: Prior to September 1985 the 19 primary schools in the district of Morley were served by one governing body comprising a chairman and a group of governors responsible for one to three schools. The chairman of this body and the school's visiting governor have been involved in this self-evaluation work since it was undertaken. They have attended relevant meetings and discussed progress, but this involvement has recently ended due to reorganisation which involves setting up new individual school governing bodies.

PARENTS: A meeting of parents was held on 18 June 1985 when the school's work on self-evaluation was explained and parents were asked if they would like to take a part (approximately 35 parents attended this meeting). The response was unanimous: everyone present was in favour. A simplified questionnaire, similar to the one filled in by the teachers, was distributed at the meeting. (Parents who did not attend the meeting were given the opportunity of filling in the questionnaire — 97 returns in all were made, approximately 30 per cent.) The survey listed 28 aspects of school life against which parents were asked to tick 'strength', 'weakness', 'satisfactory' or 'don't know'; they were also asked to make comments.

These surveys were filled in anonymously, the school providing unmarked envelopes and a central collecting box for the returns. A second meeting for parents was held in July when the survey results were distributed and comments made on the forms read out and discussed with those present. (For questionnaire and results see Appendix 2.)

The top two strengths chosen by the parents — pupil-teacher relations (60), parent-staff relations (59) — were particularly pleasing to the staff, as building good relationships has always been an important part of the ethos of the school and something all the staff have believed in and worked towards. The top weakness — methods of grouping (19) — was not unexpected, as in the last two years children in the 7–9 age group have been organised in classes with a two-year age span — something which parents have not previously experienced in the school and which, from comments on the survey form, worries them and leads me to explore the need to hold a parents meeting explaining good primary teaching and classroom organisation. From the comments on the second highest weakness — parental involvement (13) — parents were criticising those who did not support the school well, and useful discussions on how this could be improved ensued at the meeting.

Discussions on other aspects took place which could benefit from parental involvement. Links with the community and liaison between home and school were chosen. There was a request to learn about the school's work in science which scored the highest number of 'don't knows' (61), and a number of parents requested meetings to explain the school's policy on the development within subjects and across the curriculum through the school. The school intends to hold meetings on these aspects as soon as possible in the new school year.

Outcomes

The GRIDS process helped to keep the school together in working spirit when we had to vacate our main school in 1982–83. It helped us to create an atmosphere of industry, co-operation, mutual trust and honesty in the school, and enabled me, in the summer of 1984, to lead into formal staff appraisals with ease. Prior to 1984, teacher appraisals at the school had been rather incidental and informal: I was always concerned for the welfare of the staff and their personal and professional development and felt I 'knew' them very well. After discussion with LEA advisers and HMI it became clear that more could be gained if procedures were formalised and meetings arranged with staff which followed guidelines for questioning and recorded the results. Staff had previously been asked if they would welcome an opportunity for such meetings and they were unanimously in favour. Each member of staff was interviewed individually for a minimum of one hour, when job descriptions were formulated, aims, key tasks and objectives discussed, agreed and recorded, and a statement of results expected made. Praise and encouragement were given where they were due, constructive criticism where it helped teachers and the school. Personal and professional progress were discussed, and teachers made aware of their value to me and the school. We discussed their in-service needs and any contribution I and they felt they could make to our own school's in-service needs. Ways of presenting opportunities for developing their management techniques were discussed, together with how they might be involved in school policy formulation and curriculum planning. All this data was systematically assembled and recorded and a date set for further meetings to review the achievement of the key tasks and agreed objectives.

These appraisals presented a positive way of helping staff to increase their effectiveness and contribution to the school, as well as the quality of their teaching performance. There was a large element of self-appraisal both for me and the staff, and considerable in-service development of the necessary inter-personal skills, as well as considerable commitment. Each member of staff was given the opportunity to appraise me at the end of the interview. Some teachers admitted they found this difficult, mainly beccause they had never had the opportunity to do this before. After the initial embarrassment many constructive suggestions and comments were made, discussed and recorded.

Twelve months on the school is now involved in the second phase of teacher appraisals and discussions are even more valuable as we relate back to aims and objectives of a year ago and assess the progress (or lack of progress) together. I have become more aware of teachers' expertise and talents and am endeavouring to use these to the full in school life. Teachers are more frank and honest as they realise that their opinions and views matter and will be considered in staff discussions.

Since we began the GRIDS specific review study on 'Testing and assessment procedures' in February 1983, we have become increasingly aware of the necessity for improving our expertise in the evaluation of our children's work and progress. The team held discussions with two local authority psychologists who made us aware of the complexity of this process. We have endeavoured to simplify the procedures by studying each part of the curriculum systematically. The member of staff for science development, who is working closely with a LEA college of education lecturer on science, took the responsibility for evaluating the new science scheme and the methods adopted for observing and recording children's scientific progress.

He reported that:

— teachers were more confident and adventurous in their science work (one infant member of staff used battery powered circuits with the children to light up the model traffic lights, where previously coloured spots would have sufficed);

— science work was now capturing the interest of more children of all abilities (for the first time recently a group of children chose a science topic for discussion in a school assembly);

— more science displays were to be seen around school;

— children's scientific thinking had been extended:

relevant observations being made, sequential methods of working and recording, and increased ability to make predictions (a recent example — a group of five seven-year-old children working together as a team on a project on 'teeth': they ate biscuits, looked in mirrors to see where the food was trapped, transposed this information onto a plan of their teeth, interpreted the observation, discussed and recorded possible future effects on their teeth of eating too many sweet foods)!

On the first GRIDS staff survey in 1982, 12 of the 13 teachers recorded 'Work in science' to be a weakness (one abstained). On the second 1985 survey all 15 teachers recorded 'Work in science' to be 'satisfactory' — with more work still to be done: perhaps the next survey will record our science work a strength!

Earlier this year (1985) evaluative work on the maths programme, in particular the Scottish maths scheme, was devised, and the school's team reviewing testing and assessment procedures devised diagnostic tests for use at various stages in the scheme. These are now in use.

Language is the team's current evaluative study with two extra teachers joining the original group of three. We have recently begun to liaise with another LEA school which has the same ethos and philosophy as Morley Victoria. The two groups of teachers are meeting periodically to discuss and pool ideas and share expertise, whilst in the meantime continuing their own in-school discussions.

The recent PE review team's guidelines are being put into practice resulting in more thorough lesson planning and preparation: and, on observation, increased commitment by the children in their PE activities.

The LEA is currently working with its local University Department of Education to produce an evaluation of the GRIDS project within the authority. At this school we are keen to co-operate with the evaluation team as we would like to contribute towards the improvement of the GRIDS operation which has been successful in our school.

The school's work on teacher appraisal is not as advanced as the whole school self-evaluation work. Staff discussions have recently taken place on the value to the children's learning and the school of extending the existing interview form of appraisal to one similar to the seven-phase appraisal to be found on page 5 in the Suffolk teacher appraisal study[1] and paragraph 145 of *Quality in Schools*.[2] Teachers were apprehensive about the formalisation of the classroom observation

---

[1] See paper 4.1.
[2] DES. *Quality in Schools: Evaluation and Appraisal*. An HMI study. HMSO, 1985.

phase, although frank discussions on teaching skills have always taken place at the school. They thought teachers could feel threatened, undermined and demoralised, believing that their professionalism was under attack. There was a feeling that a false situation could be presented where continuity would not necessarily be obvious, some achievements would be immeasurable and teachers natural behaviour patterns might become hidden.

A worrying aspect of this extended teacher appraisal is the extra demand on the headteacher's time. The school has only fifteen hours of secretarial help, which causes many day-to-day organisational and managerial activities to be dealt with at headteacher level. With fifteen members of staff it would be advantageous to delegate some of the work to senior staff, but each of them is a class teacher and unless the staffing ratio is improved there is very little opportunity of releasing them from the classroom.

Where does the school go from here?

Evaluation and appraisal exercises will flourish in any school where the ethos and climate are right — where there is sensitive leadership and full staff consultation. Each school that undertakes them — plus the pupils and the parents it serves — will benefit, and the benefits and gains will permeate into every aspect of school life.

Morley Victoria has worked on these processes for three-and-a-half years and a number of questions arise:

— Have we effectively used the information gathered, the ideas formulated, the schemes produced?

— Have the results matched our expectations?

— Have we produced explicit criteria for evaluation?

— How do we assess whether children's learning has been improved?

Study of evaluation and appraisal techniques will continue at the school so that we can effectively answer these questions, further improve teacher performance and enhance the quality of the children's learning. The work is ongoing, the results invaluable.

Acknowledgements

The success of the work carried out in this field at Morley Victoria has been made possible by the commitment, co-operation and diligence of the teaching staff both past and present. We are also indebted for the help received from lecturers at Trinity and All Saints College, Leeds University, the LEA psychological service, and the LEA Advisory Department.

APPENDIX 1

SURVEY OF STAFF OPINION: PRIMARY SCHOOLS

Please consult the basic information paper before completing this survey sheet.

SECTION 1. Please indicate (by ticking in the appropriate column):

(i) the extent to which you feel the following aspects of the school would benefit from specific review and development;

(ii) whether you think each aspect is an area of strength or weakness or is satisfactory.

		(i)			(ii)		
		Would benefit from specific review			Strength	Satis-fac-tory	Weak-ness
		YES	NO	DON'T KNOW			
Curriculum							
Communication skills:	1. Speaking						
	2. Listening						
	3. Reading						
	4. Writing						
	5. English as a 2nd language						
Mathematics:	6. Practical						
	7. Number						
Creative work:	8. Music						
	9. Drama						
	10. Art and craft						
11. Science							
12. Topic work							
13. Physical education							
14. Personal and social development including R.E.							
15. Extra-curricular activities							
16. Continuity of the learning process 3–7							

	(i) Would benefit from specific review			(ii) Strength	Satis-fac-tory	Weak-ness
	YES	NO	DON'T KNOW			
Pupils						
17. Methods of grouping pupils						
18. Procedures for testing and assessment						
19. Pupil records, e.g. LEA record cards and internal systems						
20. Pupil reports						
21. Provision for children with special educational needs						
22. School rules and regulations						
23. Pupil-teacher relations						
Staff and organisation						
24. Staff development and in-service training arrangements						
25. Consultation and decision-making procedures						
26. Roles of responsibility-post holders						
27. Involvement of non-teaching staff						
28. Communication between staff						
29. Health and safety procedures						
30. Capitation allocation procedures						
31. Procedures relating to equipment and materials						
32. Care and maintenance of the school premises, e.g. wall displays, graffiti, litter						
33. Communication with parents						
34. Parental involvement in the school						
35. Contacts with external pupil support agencies						
36. Contacts with external professional support agencies						
37. Relationships with school governors						
38. Links with receiving schools						
39. Links with pre-school agencies						
40. Links with the community						
Please add any important topics not included above:						
41.						
42.						
43.						
44.						

SECTION 2. Bearing in mind that it may be as valuable to build on strengths as to develop areas of weakness, please select up to three aspects of school life from those listed above, including any added by you, and:

in column (i) write them below in order of priority for specific review and development within available resources <u>over the next twelve months</u>;

        (ii) explain what you mean by the topic and what the review should focus upon.

Order of priority	(i) Aspect of school life	(ii) Explanation
1		
2		
3		

Copyright © Schools Council Publications 1984

APPENDIX 2

MORLEY VICTORIA SCHOOL — SURVEY OF PARENTAL OPINION — JUNE 1985

Aspect of the school	Strength	Weak-ness	Satis-factory	Don't Know
Curriculum				
1. Reading	53	3	37	2
2. Writing	48	9	34	4
3. Mathematics	48	5	34	8
4. Music	41	5	21	26
5. Drama	12	4	29	48
6. Art and Craft	25	1	44	23
7. Science	3	7	20	61
8. Topic work (History and Geography)	9	7	28	49
9. PE	39	4	40	8
10. Personal and social development of children (RE)	13	10	43	27
11. Out of school activities	38	3	33	27
12. Continuity of learning process ($3\frac{1}{2}$–11)	43	3	29	20
Pupils, Parents, Organisation				
13. Methods of grouping pupils	12	19	36	19
14. Pupil reports	29	5	39	21
15. Provision for children with special needs	15	10	17	51
16. School rules and regulations	31	3	55	5
17. Pupil-teacher relations	60	5	28	1
18. Nursery department	36	3	18	37
19. Infant department	55	–	16	21
20. Junior department	30	1	37	25
21. School events	50	3	30	6
22. School displays	52	4	36	3
23. General tidiness (letter, etc)	46	4	42	1
24. Communication with parents	55	4	32	1
25. Parent-staff relations	59	3	28	3
26. Parental involvement in school	37	13	39	6
27. Links with the community	8	3	39	44
28. Parent Teachers' Association	13	6	53	19

The Role and Responsibility of the School

3.3 Hirst High School, Ashington, Northumberland

Richard Houlden, JP, Headmaster

A whole school assessment policy

First thoughts about the assessment of pupils dwell upon Ordinary and Advanced levels of GCE, CSE and the other external examinations which are means of recording levels of achievement at the end of courses of study. These are in this sense terminal or summative assessments and are commonly used to place young people in employment, training or higher education. These examination qualifications may be seen as the product of the educational process. Often employers seem to be looking for a simple indicator which will be applicable in many different situations. Such a universal indicator does not exist and has never existed. In the complex process of recruitment much time is required if the right placements are to be made. Consequently, it is the responsibility of the schools to provide a wide range of information which can be used by employers, higher education and various agencies to supplement examination results. All these assessments are summative products and, like the tip of an iceberg which distracts attention from the massive structure below the waves, too much attention paid to them can lead to a neglect of the formative process in school.

Education is a process of challenge, response and growth which is concerned with the individual's development in personal, academic, social and broadly vocational terms. Although the field of responsibility seems sometimes to be steadily increasing, these are the underlying concepts upon which the school's academic, recreational and pastoral or guidance curriculum is based. Of course there are the other factors of the hidden curriculum: the messages both internal and external to the school which help to form pupils' perceptions both of the school and of their futures. Often these factors are in conflict with the planned curriculum. For example, the model presented to young people may require them to work hard, achieve good examination results and so gain a good job, while youth unemployment among 16 year-old school leavers in their area is running at above 70 per cent. Consequently, peer group opinion, an important contributor to the hidden curriculum, can develop the idea that there is no future in working with the system. Even so, one hopes that when they leave school they will take with them a proper self-esteem, a willingness to contribute to their community and an understanding of their obligations to it, as well as a set of achievements. All of which reinforces the importance of formative assessments.

It is in the formative process that modification happens. The assessments may be diagnostic in order to identify and correct errors or to indicate potential; they may be designed to check that a particular concept has been mastered or a skill acquired before proceeding to the next stage; they may be designed to see whether attitudes, understanding and awareness have been developed. Whatever the formative purpose, negotiation, self-evaluation and an effective dialogue are essential here and issues are raised about teaching methods. Each school must develop a positive framework for assessment as part of a whole school assessment policy which is firmly based on the curriculum. There is no greater encouragement to commitment and sustained interest — two qualities surely essential to employers — than success and praise. A conscious effort to be achievement-orientated is what is required. That is why staged assessments, a profile of the achievement of skills and a developing record of individuals' interests and pursuits, are so important. Often a study programme designed upon this basis is organised in a modular form. That means that one complete part of the syllabus is organised as a separate unit providing for learning the appropriate facts or processes, applying them, testing the quality of the learning and recording the level of achievement. Success comes as each module of work is completed, faults can be corrected and a series of formative assessments made from what is happening in the classroom. Each stage contributes to an overall terminal assessment. The participants in the process know where they are and where they want to be. The scene is set for a progression through the course. In devising their assessment policies, teachers must have the twin objectives of positive reinforcement and progression clearly in view. Lines of progression continue after school into employment, training and further education. Can they be clearly discerned?

Very many schools are looking at these issues. While there is certainly no one correct response to them there are a number of pointers. At Hirst High School, opened in 1974 and now accommodating 1,025 pupils from 13 to 18, we have refined our policies over the years. The group tutor's role in taking an overview of an individual pupil's progress was recognised from the start and much of the task of recording achievement and assessing personal qualities falls to them under the guidance of their head of house. An active Curriculum Development Committee (CDC) provides a means of discussing policy matters: curriculum papers have been issued under its aegis and it has helped to develop a consensus among the staff over purposes and objectives. A deliberate and active policy for in-service training was and is closely related to CDC discussions, while for the last five years a process of Departmental Review has been used to assess our achievement. Our response is developing and changing not least through the operation of working parties to review particular matters and present reports to the whole teaching staff.

The GCSE recognises in theory the wider assessment considerations outlined above. Particularly welcome will be the move away from norm-referencing when criteria-related grades are introduced. The development of these criteria will give pupils clear yardsticks against which to measure themselves. Schools will need to modify their syllabuses to respond to the criteria, but must avoid a rigid adherence to a new orthodoxy which might otherwise become just as stultifying as the old one. It remains to be seen whether an effective programme of in-service training can be provided in the time before the first candidates sit GCSE and whether it can be sustained over the following years. In-service training of quality is going to be essential if GCSE is to meet its own criteria as an examination system.

Academic assessments are not the only ones to be made in schools. Measured in terms of current GCE standards the more stringent academic targets are not within the reach of 75 per cent of pupils. The challenge facing all certification is to provide appropriate targets for a large part, some might argue all, of the ability range. Standards can be raised but teachers' time will become an issue in the process. For example, improvement will require the development of facilitative teaching methods. Such methods rely on extensive dialogue with individuals, on the negotiation of objectives and assessments, and on enquiry methods of learning; and they aim essentially to nurture understanding rather than to top up the recipient with factual information. The extent to which they can be achieved with the pupil : teacher ratios currently available in many LEAs must be open to question. The didactic method is well suited to large classes and the passing on of information. To move away from it without the ability to create smaller teaching groups will be difficult. However, even if the new examination system provides better targets there must also be assessment of those other qualities which schools seek to foster.

No one who has completed references for school leavers can be in any doubt that teachers do assess the personal qualities of pupils. The question which arises is, how are these assessments to be made? It is very difficult to define criteria for the assessment of personal qualities: such assessments are, and must remain, subjective, depending on the professional judgement of teachers. That is why the exercise should be an open one in which both pupils and parents have an opportunity to contribute to records kept by the pastoral organisation. While there is no simple answer as to what should be assessed, our present assessments are shown in Appendix 1 which is a copy of the profile given to everyone at 16-plus. It was developed in this form by a working party and it superseded a very dated 'leaving profile', which we had used for the previous five years. No doubt it in turn will be replaced as our perceptions and assessment abilities improve.

Meantime, it comments on the ten areas most frequently asked about by employers, was agreed with the Careers Advisory Service and was discussed with the Parent-Teachers' Association.

Most examining boards are working on some kind of record of achievement. The Oxford Certificate of Educational Achievement and the Northern Examining Association's Record of Achievement are two examples. For a school to provide its own profile in addition to participating in one administered by an examination board would be unnecessary duplication. Whatever the type of profile, teacher time is again a major problem. Even for such a relatively limited record as the profile which we provide, the demands made of staff are very considerable. For at the formative stage information is recorded about school examinations, field courses, expeditions, team membership, referrals for commendation or punishment; in fact a mass of information upon which the profile can be based. It is, however, highly regarded by the pupils and well used by the employers who remember to ask for it. Every effort should be made to make the record a positive one. It should record achievement and should be based on a picture accumulated throughout a school career so that the faults associated with subjective assessments may be avoided. The summative final assessment is not the hasty contrivance of one individual but a considered summary based on open, recorded observations over the years. There have been some demands for a 'warts and all document', which records faults, weaknesses and misdemeanours. 'Stole 50p in the First Year' might sum up this approach, which is surely unnecessarily punitive, for there must be some possibility of redemption! The system should encourage young people to build on what they have achieved rather than damn them for past mistakes.

More work needs to be done on the development of appropriate targets for those for whom an external examinations system is not appropriate. Appendix 2 shows the pre-vocational studies profile which we use for this propose. The completion of the summative profile is the responsibility of the pre-vocational studies tutor who co-ordinates the study programme and the work of a team of teachers drawn from all areas of the curriculum. The section headed 'Pupil's comment' in the profile gives crude and all too brief recognition to the role that pupils play in making assessments on the course.

There is a consensus emerging about many aspects of pupil assessment, despite the difficulties of teacher time and the need to explain the system and train new members of the team as staff gain promotions to other schools. It is the responsibility of schools and of the teaching profession to develop new systems of assessment, but if that is to happen the development must be properly resourced with time for in-service training. That sets the scene for the appraisal of teachers.

There is much justification for trying to find means of rewarding effective teachers, but it is important to remember that this description fits the majority in the profession. In this sense teacher assessment got off to a bad start, 'Appraisal by law threat to teachers', as one newspaper headline put it. Teacher appraisal is not about using a disciplinary stick and no-one would wish to devise an appraisal system around the very small number of teachers who may require firm action. For them it is possible to use a check-list to consider issues like punctuality and the suitability of work, which can lead, if it is appropriate, to their facing the governors with an adverse report. Such procedures exist already and what is required is the decision to use them. While trying to find means of rewarding effective teachers it is important to remember that secondary schools in particular have a hierarchy of responsibilities which is essential to the effective management of the educational process. It may be necessary to assess the hierarchy and to rearrange it, but it cannot be discarded.

In practice, however informally, schools do assess teachers for promotion and, indeed, it is one of the prime responsibilities of senior management to develop the potential of their staffs. In this sense assessment for salary purposes is appropriate. It is similarly appropriate as a preparation for the move from the entry grade, envisaged under current proposals, to the main professional grade after a suitable induction programme. However, there is no scope for anything akin to a production bonus. This is because the educational process is not a mechanical one in which the quality and quantity of the product is solely dependent on the operative's skill and effort. Pupils are not all of equal ability, parental support is not universal, and individuals grow and develop at different rates. Salary matters are not the main reason for teacher assessment.

Teacher appraisal is to assess how far schools and their departments have defined appropriate objectives and met those objectives in relation to improving pupil performance. It is about the quality of the educational process. Today's pressing issues are those of teaching style and the nature of the dialogue in the classroom. In fact, just those issues which are important in pupil appraisal. That is why it is very difficult to devise clear criteria which are tightly related to a scale of performance. One is analysing the quality of the relationships not the *product* of a mechanised system. Nonetheless many schools have devised appraisal models and the one we have used for the past five years in this school is termed 'Professional development and performance review'.

This system grew out of our 'Policy for in-service training'. Having run much school-based in-service we were concerned to see how effective it was and what more was required and, similarly, having set up systems with which to operate a new school we wanted to see how well they were working. The review is organised in departmental units and the main steps are these:

a. *First there is an extensive discussion between the head of department and a designated deputy headteacher, in which ideas are generated.* These discussions are concerned with the operation of the department. What are its current aims and objectives? What has its performance been in relation to these aims? What are its examination results like? What is the resource situation in the department? What developments are required? These issues are very fully discussed with all in the department before the written report is produced with the designated deputy headteacher's help.

b. *There follow written reports on each teacher in the department outlining the range of classes taught and determining in-service requirements.* The process is an open one in which everyone has access to the review and there are no secret documents.

c. *The final report is presented to me as headmaster by the head of department and there follow individual appraisal interviews with each teacher.* The detailed instructions for the 1985 professional development and performance review are given in Appendix 3.

The strengths of this system are manifold. The managerial role of the head of department is reinforced and extended, and the deputy headteachers are brought into a close examination of the work of the departments for which they are responsible. There is therefore an important element of in-service training here. The reports on individuals, as well as those on departments, are used to plan school-based training programmes, to prepare for applications to external courses and to assess the need for internal and external secondments.

Put generally, the principles are these:

a. *First, the objective is to improve the quality of the educational experience for young people.* Unlike the previous generation of teachers, this generation has to accept the fact that change is one of the constants with which they have to cope. Unless this factor is recognised and faced they will be forced back on outdated procedures, the security of the GCE O-level syllabus and the shelter of the didactic method.

b. *If the biggest issue facing the profession is that of teaching style and the development of alternative strategies for teaching, then the second objective of appraisal is to provide reinforcement for professional development.* Such professional development will require collaboration between teachers to assess their own needs and determine their directions in accordance with the broad objectives of the educational system. That in turn will place great demands on the team leaders who are the managers of the process.

c. *The third objective of teacher appraisal is therefore the enhancement of the management role.*

If these three objectives are put together in the system, then appraisal will help to develop and sustain a self-energising debate about our purposes. It will also create, at any rate, at an institutional level, a common sense of purpose, and it will help provide the flexibility essential if we are to cope with the challenge of change. Such, at any rate, is the rationalisation five years on. It was not all quite so clear at the start.

There are weaknesses in the system. Although no member of staff has ever quibbled about being reviewed because it is seen as a positive process, some heads of department have been reluctant to pass judgement. What, after all, are the criteria to be used? This problem has been met to some extent by the collaborative nature of the exercise between deputy headteacher and head of department and by the fact that its open nature lends itself to a constructive and properly critical dialogue. There is also the problem of how to deal with relatively young teachers who are clearly in terminal appointments. How does one go on reviewing them? Here planned in-service and internal secondments provide part of the answer.

Has teacher appraisal improved the process for the pupils? Teachers are much more aware of the important issues facing them about teaching style and method. Many have or are adopting new approaches. New courses have been developed. Consequently, the answer to my question must be 'yes', but it is not quantifiable in terms of results or attitudes.

Schools are, of course, appraised in other ways. There are HMI inspections which provide a pretty thorough account of individual institutions, as do the reports of the LEA's advisers. The headteacher presents regular reports to governors, and many schools issue an annual report of the school's activities to parents and governors, which, like a company's annual report, goes into considerable detail about performance. These forms of institutional review are well established and their mention here serves as a necessary reminder to those who think appraisal is something new for schools.

The ideas contained in this paper are neither new nor unique, although the extent to which they have been brought together in the practice of one school may represent a significant development. Our pupil assessments need refinement and a clearer analysis of criteria, and while teacher reviews certainly assist professional development, heads of department and all teachers need more time to get into their colleagues' classrooms.

Any school can start on developing its assessment policies providing the pre-conditions for change exist. These include an open management style and an outward-looking philosophy which help to neutralize the threats assumed to be implicit in the concept of appraisal. The principles upon which the appraisal of pupils and teachers are based are very much the same. The need is for positive evaluations to be used alongside criteria-related academic assessments for pupils, because it is attitude, commitment and values, as well as academic performance, which are important to society at large. For teachers, too, a positive framework for appraisal is essential because it provides the key to staff development and the improvement of the service. For all in schools assessment should be an open exercise and one which is integral to the educational process. Teachers should know it is going on and be invited to contribute to it.

Learning is a process, not a product. In the final analysis appraisal is about the quality of that process. If that is right, then the product will be a good one. The principle to bear in mind is that we should educate people for what they might have the capacity to become and so not be content with objectives which are solely instrumental.

Appendix 1 (opposite) is a facsimile of the profile given to pupils of Hirst High School during their final year of compulsory education.
Appendix 2 (p133) is a facsimile of the school's pre-vocational studies profile.

APPENDIX I

HIRST HIGH SCHOOL
PROFILE
for

_____

R. Houlden J.P. B.A.
Headmaster

This document is issued to pupils during their final year of compulsory education in the school, and it may be used as an open testimonial. Should a confidential reference be required giving more specific details about the pupil, the Headmaster will be pleased to supply this upon request.

It is expected that pupils will present this document in conjunction with examination certificates and/or a P.V.S. profile.

SUBJECTS STUDIED	LEVEL TO WHICH SUBJECT WAS STUDIED

This pupil has also followed courses in Personal Development Studies and Physical Education.

INTERESTS, ACHIEVEMENTS and COURSES

COMMENTS

Head of House:

APPEARANCE		Always takes a pride in appearance
		Usually well presented
		Well presented on occasions
		Could take more pride in appearance
INDUSTRY and PERSEVERANCE		Always conscientious and persevering
		Generally hard-working and persevering
		Makes some effort, but occasionally gives up
		Lacks determination and makes little effort
SOCIABILITY		Outgoing, friendly manner
		Usually forms good relationships
		Appears to be shy, or reluctant to make friends
		Has difficulty in establishing relationships
COOPERATION with OTHER PUPILS		Always works well with others
		Usually works well with others
		Occasionally works well with others
		Rarely works well with others
COOPERATION with STAFF		Always helpful and willing
		Usually cooperative
		Can be cooperative on occasions
		Rarely helpful or willing
COURTESY		Always courteous and well-mannered
		Generally courteous and well-mannered
		Can be courteous and well-mannered on occasions
		Rarely courteous or well-mannered
ORAL SKILLS		A confident, fluent speaker who is easily understood
		Generally communicates clearly
		At times communicates satisfactorily, but is often hesitant
		Reluctant to speak or has difficulty communicating effectively
RELIABILITY and RESPONSIBILITY		Utterly reliable and accepts responsibility well
		Dependable and willing to accept responsibility
		Can be relied upon in certain situations
		Can be unreliable
CONFIDENCE		Confident and self-assured
		Usually confident
		Can show confidence on occasions
		Lacks confidence and self-assurance
PRACTICAL SKILLS		Always works with skill and confidence in practical areas
		Generally works with skill and confidence
		Has some practical ability, but needs guidance or encouragement
		Lacks skill or confidence

ATTENDANCE
IN
19 — 19

PUNCTUALITY

Excellent
Good
Poor

Headmaster _____

131

BACK COVER OF THE HIRST HIGH SCHOOL PROFILE

APPENDIX 2

HIRST HIGH SCHOOL

PRE-VOCATIONAL STUDIES PROFILE 198 -8

or _____

STUDY PROGRAMME

1. _____	4. _____
2. _____	5. _____
3. _____	6. _____

R. HOULDEN, J.P. B.A.
Headmaster

Keenness and Effort	Needs some encouragement and guidance	
	Tries hard when interested.	
	Always willing, occasionally needs encouragement.	
	Always enthusiastic and willing.	
Working with Other Pupils	Finds difficulty in working with other pupils.	
	Works well with pupils of own choice.	
	Usually works well with other pupils.	
	Will work well with all other pupils.	
Working with Adults	Can follow instructions for simple tasks with guidance.	
	Can follow spoken instructions and complete tasks independently	
	Works effectively with minimum of instruction.	
	Inspires confidence and communicates well with adults.	
Behaviour	Shows some lapses in self-discipline.	
	Disciplined and polite when supervised.	
	Usually self-disciplined and courteous.	
	Always self-disciplined and polite.	
Talking and Listening	Can relay a simple, verbal message.	
	Can give descriptions and explanations.	
	Talks to most people in different situations.	
	Responds as a confident, fluent speaker.	
Reading and Writing	Can write and understand simple material.	
	Can give and understand straight forward written explanations.	
	Uses specialised material and responds in writing.	
	Criticises written work and uses it to produce own writing.	
Visual Understanding	Can follow simple signs and indicators.	
	With help can use basic charts, forms etc.	
	Understands basic charts etc. unaided.	
	Produces own visual material.	
Using Equipment	After being shown, can use equipment safely to do simple tasks.	
	With help can use equipment to do harder tasks.	
	Selects and uses the right equipment for the job.	
	Uses and looks after equipment. Can identify/remedy faults.	
Manual Skills	Can handle simple equipment as shown.	
	Can reliably carry out practical tasks.	
	Can carry out more complicated practical tasks.	
	Can carry out tasks needing a high level of skill.	

	Can read scales and dials.	
Measuring	Can measure out materials.	
	Can set up and use simple measuring instruments.	
	Can set up and use complex measuring instruments.	
	Can identify size, shape, order etc.	
Calculating	Can +/− whole numbers. Uses a calculator with help.	
	Can +/−/x/÷ to solve single step problems with a calculator.	
	Can solve two step problems and can estimate.	
	Takes part in most sports.	
Sports Skills	Takes part in most sports and has done well in some.	
	Is a keen sports person, tries to do well in most sports.	
	Is physically skilled, keen on most sports.	
	Needs continuous help.	
Planning	Needs intial help, then occasional guidance.	
	Can work independently, but needs some support.	
	Works independently and resourcefully.	
	Needs help in researching from a single source.	
Information Seeking	Needs help in researching from a variety of sources.	
	Needs help to use researched material.	
	Independently collects and uses information.	
	With help can cope with simple problems.	
Coping with Problems	Can cope in familiar situations with some support.	
	Shows initiative in most situations.	
	Copes even in unfamiliar situations.	
	I do not agree with any of this report.	
Pupil's Comment	I only agree with some of this report.	
	I agree with most of this report.	
	I agree with all of this report.	
Staff Comments		

135

COMMUNITY SERVICE

WORK EXPERIENCE

LINK COURSES

QUALIFICATIONS

Headmaster: _____

APPENDIX 3

PROFESSIONAL DEVELOPMENT AND PERFORMANCE REVIEW 1985

INTRODUCTION

These reviews must be undertaken bearing in mind;

    a. the need to respond to HMI's recommendations;

       and

    b. the need to respond to the County Curriculum Document.

Please remember these are working documents and they should, therefore, be explicit and brief. These reviews cover the past year and look forward two years.

THE HEADINGS AND SUB-SECTIONS

A. i. Aims — General

    ii. Objectives — Particular

B. Resources

    i. Capitation and text books/materials, with particular relevance to the current situation in the Department.

    ii. Rooms and furniture

    iii. Audio-visual aids, etc.

C. Staffing

    i. Range and quality of staff — any GREAT strengths and SIGNIFICANT gaps or weaknesses?

    ii. Any 'in-service' required?

    iii. Any messages for future directions?

    iv. Any comment on ancillary support — where appropriate?

D. Have the Department's broad aims and particular objectives been met?

E. Have the 'outcomes' of the Department's courses been up to standard?

    i. Profiled results

    ii. Internal terminal assessments or formative ones.

    iii. Public examination results (to be completed in September).

THE STAFF REVIEW

Remember our aim here is to be positive. We wish to build on strengths rather than to expose weaknesses. The suggestion is that teachers start their own assessments by wiriting their own reviews, which are then discussed with Heads of Department to produce a final version. To be included are:

    i. The range of classes taught.

    ii. The contribution to the department as a whole?

    iii. Future directions and training? In-service implications?

iv. Any gaps to be filled or any weaknesses to be worked on over the next two years?

v. Any personal views about the department or school?

CONCLUSION

The process of our review is a consultative one: Heads of Department with Deputies, and members of the Department with Head of Department, in order to produce the review. The final stage is the personal interview with the Headmaster.

The Role and Responsibility of the School

3.4 Putteridge High School and Community College, Luton

Albert Price, Headteacher

The foundation of quality appraisal and assessment within the school system must reside within a clear statement of educational philosophy and principle as a basis of intent towards all pupils since without this any appraisal lacks specific purpose. These principles in education must be known and recognised by us all not just teachers, as the touchstone against which aims and objectives are identified, and decisions, actions, strategies are judged. Within a school the responsibility rests with the staff to ensure that the philosophy and principles are understood and applied in policy and practice at all levels. Outside a school the responsibility is to support such activity. This contract of ideals identifies the degree of liberty and restraint which is rightly a teacher's professional freedom in attending to the needs of individual pupils and the community of pupils. The regular exposition of agreed principles within and around a school enables individual and corporate judgments to be made about the degree of success and achievement as we translate aims into activity. Appraisal and assessment now become positive exercises into which motivation and initiative will flow. If attitudes towards appraisal and assessment are to be what they can be, then there also has to be an encouragement and acceptance of more participation and shared management in schools which in turn requires significant changes in traditional roles including that of the headteacher — changes in policies for resourcing schools, for professional development and curriculum innovation.

Putteridge High School is an 11–16 mixed comprehensive school and community college built 10 years ago. It has a pupil population of 1,100 with 60 teaching staff. It serves an area to the south of Luton on the Bedfordshire/ Hertfordshire border.

The principles which underpin education at Putteridge High School are that:

    i. education is a moral transaction;

    ii. the equal value of persons is respected in their right to be fully educated;

    iii. each pupil has infinite learning potential;

   iv. different learning responses determine what is made of opportunity not the extent of opportunity;

   v. all knowledge exists — it simply awaits discovery;

   vi. educational opportunity needs to be infinite in character and availability to match the infinite nature of potential;

   vii. discrimination in opportunity by ability is immoral — as it is by race, creed or colour;

   viii. the principle of entitlement to unconditional opportunity is a pre-condition to the quest for improving standards;

   ix. education is meant to unite and not to divide.

On the basis of these principles we define a comprehensive school as one which continually seeks to ensure that opportunity is so organised that through its teachers, curriculum and total resources it offers unconditionally all that it provides at all times to all pupils and staff.

If the above type of school is to be developed and the above principles to be pursued, then evaluation of the progress made is more than a procedure in a network of activity. It is a process, even an attitude, which operates throughout the cycle of planning, resourcing, teaching, development and assessment and leads to constant self- and corporate evaluation which we need to emphasise; an awareness and acceptance that we are all professionally accountable to ourselves, each other and our pupils. Awareness of responsibility heightens concern for standards and encourages the process of self-critical evaluation. This attitude thrives only in a suitable environment which rests primarily in the creation of recognisable and agreed principles promoted by effective structures, organisation and management within and surrounding the school. Where these exist the concept of self-evaluation is a feature likely to prove most fruitful and positive.

Three clusters of strategies

There are strategies which contribute to this attitude of constant self-evaluation and which enable teachers to know each other as professional colleagues, aware of agreed corporate principles and standards. The strategies employed at Putteridge High School fall into three dimensions: those concerned with provision, those concerned with response and those concerned with reporting.

In the first cluster of strategies are:

— management documents

— communication and consultation

— in-service training

— staffing structures

— resource policies

— the teaching climate

A school management document sets out educational principle establishing whole school policies for the conduct of the curriculum and all related management matters. Each school area is required to produce compatible management documents, in response to the school document, which provide a more specific statement of how principles and policies are translated into aims and objectives, strategies, syllabuses, schemes of work, assessment, etc. These documents establish a framework around which the work of individuals and groups of teachers can develop. For experienced staff the schemes of work represent the common ground of content, skills or values to which pupils require access and upon which their efforts will be appraised and their achievement assessed. Inexperienced staff, and those new to the school, require this as part of the structure of their induction into the life of the school. Their supervision requires regular, personal contact with the head of department, with pastoral colleagues and with the supervising deputy or senior teacher to gain support, advice and encouragement.

Teachers' ease of access to their immediate managers, head of department, year head, deputies and headteacher is carefully organised. A structure of communication, consultation and participation exists through a regular timetabled meeting programme. Provision is made for access to colleagues at any level, without being restricted by a hierarchic management structure. The head is always available, is seen around the school and the environs of the school and especially in the playground and staffroom. The teachers are encouraged towards a 'high school profile' as well as a 'high classroom profile'. The pattern of meetings are channels for communication and consultation, and all such meetings have agendas and minutes in order that such objectives may be achieved. Items which pass through such meetings offer the opportunity for encouragement of consistency by all staff and the opportunity for full involvement. The meetings are used for matters of curriculum, staff and pupil development, avoiding the temptation to become purely administrative or instructive. Constructive and stimulating meetings provide stimulus for the corporate evaluation of performance at various levels. The care given to in-service provision is an essential feature of the teaching climate. We identify the needs of the school and of the teachers, and assess how both internal and external in-service activities and programmes can be used to promote curriculum development and improve personnel. Within the school the annual school conference (now in its tenth year) illustrates a most effective approach to the identification and development of needs in priority areas of school activity. The programme is planned and developed throughout the year prior to the staff weekend conference. This is the culmination of planning and its fruits will subsequently be introduced into the life of the school in the year ahead. It is a continuous evaluation of 'where we are now' and an attempt to sustain our 'vision of the future'.

It is important that in-service training programmes are seen as an important resource ranking with capitation, the number of teachers and the state of the accommodation. Each in-service release is viewed from the perspectives of school development and teacher development: and this is done by the staff. Release for one of their members has to be a decision shared by a group of colleagues in response to a need in their working area and valuable to the individual involved. Teachers need to share and benefit from the training experiences of their colleagues and this is achieved by participation in every part of the process. Each area of the school is asked to establish, through consultation, its own priorities and to promote its own programme within the context of its management document.

Schools need salary structure policies; how this is managed is an important feature of the teaching climate of the school and the response of teachers to it. The policy reflects the importance of each part of the school curriculum and organisation to the life of the whole school. The policy is stated and followed so that teachers see an appreciation of their work reflected in promotion prospects which are not over-valued or devalued. To appoint a head of department to a Scale 2, provide no curriculum base and no other colleagues, allocate one lesson a week, give a highly competitive position on curriculum choice forms, is to ridicule the curriculum, the teacher and the pupils. There is no climate for evaluation and assessment. The value placed upon each separate curriculum activity and upon the personnel involved is also clearly reflected within policies allocating other essential resources; ie. capitation, accommodation, teaching and support staff and in-service opportunity. Too often lack of care in these matters and absence of principle, demotivates and disillusions teachers. The result is a deteriorating teaching climate.

Within the climate created the school finds a positive approach and attitude by its teachers to every aspect of school life. There is a pupil/colleague/school consciousness which stimulates individual initiative and fosters co-operative activity.

The introduction of new teachers to the full life of a school is more difficult than the introduction of new pupils and is achieved by careful planning. They need to see the more experienced and skilfull teachers managing the classroom situation as well as be seen teaching themselves.

There is also a need for all teachers to see a range of teaching across the curriculum of the school: it is valuable to see groups of children at work in teaching situations other than ones own. It also gives an insight into the 'whole' school life of pupils which assists assessment of pupil performance in a particular aspect of school life and contributes to the ethos of the school. This policy encourages an attitude in both staff and pupils that we do not work in isolation and contributes to our own security and our acceptance of each other. Such openness is further developed by encouraging teachers to teach with 'open doors'.

The second cluster of strategies, ie. *those concerned with response include:*

— role definition

— role appraisal

— role exchange and role change

— staff profiling

The needs of the school and the department/year, the current stage of curriculum development, the strengths of individual teachers and the composition of the team all contribute to the production of role definitions. A willingness to continually review, update and even change roles within a school and departments allow for a professional response to current directions in school policy and for development in professional skill and expertise. This is achieved by involving staff in their own role definitions and by requiring each role to reflect the whole task of the school and attend to the development of the teacher. Each role has three essential elements: administration, curriculum development and pastoral care. The teacher is to be developed as a manager in a comprehensive school, and as soon as that process begins the role emphasises specific responsibilities and whole school awareness. This continues and increases at each stage of promotion. The compatibility of roles within the groupings of teachers, is accompanied with a requirement on each group for regular agreement about standards and expectations, and the need for direction and encouragement for those with less experience. A team approach to planning is essential to the corporate attitudes we seek, and to the responsible release of the individual flair and initiative which exists as something of value to others. This team approach is reflected in syllabus planning, lesson preparation, presentation, evaluation and assessment. Team teaching also exists as one approach used in the majority of departments. This offers further opportunity for the monitoring of teaching styles and the improvement of practice.

Aims and objectives are re-stated annually within a consultative framework involving all staff. Goals are established within departments which are evaluated continuously, periodically or at least annually, according to expectation and experience. Each teacher is expected to provide personal aims and objectives for their immediate manager and to critically review past performance. Personal interviews occur within this procedure and each staff member is also interviewed by the headteacher twice in each school year. By taking advantage of the positive attitude created, these processes also help to emphasise the value of each individual contribution within the whole school's attempt to translate principles into practice.

At a time of low teacher mobility and reduced external promotion it is important that internal opportunities are advertised within a school. There is always a need for teachers to offer themselves for promotion — to assess their own readiness and to evaluate themselves. They are helped to do this by procedures established by the senior teacher in charge of professional development. This is preferable to 'behind closed doors' procedures, is much more open and encouraging to the staff. This internal advertising will include all the normal procedures for teacher appointments. Teachers are also required to change management roles, especially senior staff who are awaiting promotion in an environment where opportunities are limited. This strategy, which requires very considerate management technique, encourages continued development and creates openings for younger teachers with expectations of recognition for their initiative and effort. The teachers are encouraged to keep their own profiles: ie. a chronological record of their own growth in academic qualifications and in management experience. Their own view on how they see their career and its related needs are clearly expressed along with a critical analysis of their year-by-year objectives and achievement. This profile is always included in a teacher/headteacher interview and may in the future be based upon a more 'open-file' reference system.

The third cluster of strategies are concerned with recording and reporting

Evaluation is recorded and this too is an activity in which all participate. Each manager is required to produce a written evaluation of the work of their area based upon reports and interviews with colleagues. These are combined with governors' reports. Also included are evaluative progress reports on those aspects of school life which need improving and those which are doing well. An 'end of year' booklet is produced and circulated, helping to strengthen the corporate approach to evaluation and to sustain enthusiasm for the principles of the school and vigour in the strategies being developed to promote them.

The school encourages external evaluation both by its clients and by professional agencies. Although visited by Inspectors and Advisers we also invite them, in order to capitalise upon an important resource. Similar resources are available from colleges and universities. We also learn from other schools and opportunities to visit or be visited are grasped. We seek to expand the limited traditional view of parents and employers: ie. open days, work displays, speech days, report evenings, PTA. Whilst using some of these we seek to extend the involvement of these adults into the work and life of the school. We have a PPTA

(Parent, Pupil, Teacher Association) whose policy is to generate understanding of the school through working curriculum situations for parents, employers, pupils and teachers. Every Monday evening we have a regular attendance of 200-plus adults and pupils on a programme generated around the curriculum, pastoral care, careers and teaching techniques.

Many people ask questions of teachers regarding performance, pupil achievement and school discipline. Too often, at present, when teachers are questioned they feel threatened. A fruitful evaluation process does not begin until teachers question themselves. This requires confidence and security, involvement and enthusiasm. These are not strong features in today's teaching force. Teachers are not encouraged to question themselves whilst confusion exists about the purposes of education and of schools; this is compounded by resource policies which frustrate the commitment of teachers and the quality of their work. Nor can they be sure of their role and responsibility to the learner in how to prepare, present and assess until there is a clearer relationship between these activities and the agreed purposes of education. This relationship at present does not exist. There are too many conflicts in the expectations placed upon teachers and too many insensitive sectional interests operating around schools for teachers to be other than defensive. When teachers are held accountable they are too frequently the victims of conditions created within their working environment by those who seek to assess them. It is worrying that many of the present encouragements towards improved evaluation of teacher performance and assessment of pupil response seem to have their beginnings, at least partially, in the belief that there is something extra that can be squeezed out of teachers to compensate for that which is lacking in finance and resources. There is a suspicion that the present pressure has its origins in a conviction that teachers are inefficient and any under performance by pupils results solely from this. In such an environment, evaluation and inspection of schools demotivates rather than encourages. Appraisal and inspection are just more wounding experiences. The conflicts which exist are highlighted, the progress which is sought is diminished. Self-evaluation can only begin from a confident professional plateau. Evaluation will not gain support until those responsible for the teacher condition in schools are also subjected to critical evaluation.

This moves us forward to an examination of pupil performance and to consider the purposes of assessment and the factors which influence judgement. It is important to acknowledge the pupil condition as a pre-requisite of their readiness to learn. Pupils need so much more than intellectual ability, good teachers and up-to-date resources to succeed in school. Pupils bring to school different levels of response to learning affected by many external factors which are outside immediate teacher influence or control.

Within a school any assessment should help a teacher to identify the strengths and weaknesses in the achievement of an individual pupil. It needs to cover adequately the range of skills, activities, concepts and attitudes to which a pupil is expected to respond both in the formal and the informal teaching situations. Not only should it help to motivate pupil response in terms of the formal curriculum and the school ethos but it should also make a major contribution to the evaluation of the effectiveness and the suitability of the courses being taught, and the effectiveness of the school's attempts in the creation of its atmosphere: ie. it can reflect the need both for corporate re-adjustment by teachers and the individual teacher's need for future planning and preparation.

There is a need for a variety of techniques which include not only marks, grades, and awards, but also oral and written encouragement in class comment, the marking of books, and, in general, contact, to try to ensure that pupils can give a positive response to their work and environment and lead to their own self-evaluation.

Adequate records need to be kept on a pupil's progress to produce a cumulative record of achievement, both written and oral, which to parents should be meaningful and comprehensive. The quality of the profile should be judged by the success achieved in the build-up of knowledge of the pupil response to learning translated into improved teacher techniques and strategies. But it should be remembered that pupils are also influenced by factors outside the school which will be reflected in their response to what the school offers.

We must not lose sight of the prime objective in evaluation and assessment: the improvement of teacher:pupil relationships in the school situation and an improvement in educational standards. It is too easy to concentrate upon the quality and detail of records, too attractive to segment continuously pupils like oranges, and to break skills down into meaningless detail. The quality of a profile is not to be judged by the thickness of a file or even the value to an employer, but by the success achieved in the build-up of knowledge of the pupil response to learning translated into improved teacher techniques and strategies and improved pupil performance. Do the teachers know more about the pupils and the ways in which they learn? Do the pupils learn more effectively? These should be the prime objectives of assessment and evaluation.

More children fail in school due to a lack of personal security and a state of personal unhappiness than lack of ability. No pupil can perform in such a condition whatever the expertise and care of the teacher or the quality of the environment and provision of resources. At present up to 35 per cent of pupils are in broken homes and this condition is no respecter of intellectual capacity. Before the education service rushes into a rash judgement about standards it is important to recognise the condition of the pupils and to identify the reasons and responsibility for that condition. It is also unacceptable to expect schools to maintain standards, values and attitudes to work and responsibility which are not supported by public activity in society itself. The total environment surrounding young people is educative, for good or bad, and directly influences their attitude to schools, and to teachers and also the personal performance of the pupils. Learning is not simply cognitive but is also affective; indeed if it is not both then neither thrives. Learning in school cannot be identified purely as an exercise generated between schoolteacher and school pupil. Teachers contribute to the learning process, but when a pupil is assessed then the contributions of all influences are assessed.

APPENDIX 1

ASSESSMENT OF PUPIL PERFORMANCE

Purposes of assessment

1. *Diagnostic assessment.* Suitable assessment techniques undertaken continuously or periodically can enable a teacher to identify strengths and weaknesses in the achievement of an individual pupil.

   a. This requires the regular monitoring of classwork and homework in ways which reveal areas of work in which a pupil is already succeeding, or difficulties which are being experienced.

   b. Diagnostic assessment assumes that the results will be used by teachers to structure their future work with pupils. Planning and preparation need to be flexible enough to respond to the results of such assessment.

   c. To be of maximum value techniques are needed which are discriminatory (in terms of content or skills), immediate and precise.

2. *Motivation by assessment.* Is pupil performance improved because of the existence of assessment tests, book marking, verbal encouragement, extended tuition, reports to parents, grading of classwork, commendation awards, etc? Each of these implies that an assessment of current progress is being made and used in an appropriate way. What are your pupils' responses to your monitoring of their work?

   a. The suggestion here is that a variety of techniques of assessment is required if the full range of motivation-stimuli is to be exploited.

   b. Care must also be taken if assessment is not to become a demotivator for certain individuals or groups.

   c. How we USE assessment results may be as important as the results themselves.

3. *Classifying by assessment.* This is the primary purpose of external examinations. Pupils may also be ranked in relation to each other on the basis of their performance in continuous or terminal assessments. We may require a classification of current pupil achievement when constructing teaching groups or preparing entry lists for examinations.

   a. Are our classifications or 'orders of merit' based upon sufficient, reliable evidence?

   b. Are these classifications flexible enough to respond to changes in pupil achievement?

   c. How do we avoid the danger of our classifications becoming self-fulfilling — encouraging a pupil to respond at the level of expectation which we appear to have set?

   d. Are our current assessment procedures, within the department, adequate for the preparation of external examination entries?

   e. At what stage, and for what reasons, do we need to classify pupils according to ability or achievement?

4. *Assessment and parents.* It is our stated aim in school that '. . . parents can expect, through information and consultation, the school to be respectful of their opinions and attitudes. . .' and that '. . . the school should foster the understanding of parents in these (including assessment) matters. . .'

If the contributions of school and home are to be integrated to pursue a common purpose then information needs to be made available to parents by the school.

   a. Homework tasks may be set with which parents can be involved.

   b. Pupils can be encouraged to discuss their classwork and their assessment results with their parents.

   c. Commendation awards provide an interim recognition of success and of worthwhile achievement.

   d. Reports to parents should be meaningful and comprehensive, particularly the written comments.

   e. The school has the responsibility to contribute continuously to parental understanding of the system and clarification of the information provided.

   f. Parents expect our assessment to include an identifiable measure of achievement.

5. **Evaluation by assessment.** Assessment of pupil performance can make a major contribution to the evaluation of our courses and teaching methods. This use of assessment is not intended to make us accountable to external agencies, but rather to yield information about the suitability of our courses — an internal departmental exercise. Rowntree[1] proposes a cyclic model which helps to show the part played by assessment in the teaching process:

---

[1] Rowntree D (1977). *Assessing Students: How shall we know them?* London: Harper & Row.

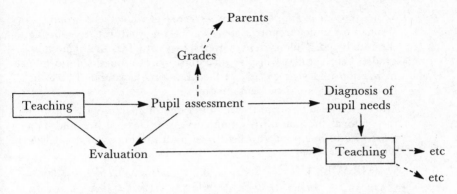

a. Which aspects of our assessment programme are most likely to aid evaluation of our teaching methods, eg. test results, pupil response, attitudes? etc.

b. Do we adjust our teaching strategies in the light of assessment results?

c. Departments may wish to adopt strategies for evaluation of internal and external assessment/examination results in response to the school evaluation document.

What do we assess?

Assessment needs to be related to the objectives of each department. The assessment booklet indicates how departments have approached the analysis of their work for assessment purposes.

a. The key question is... 'do our assessment techniques adequately cover the range of skills, activities, concepts and attitudes which our objectives aim to teach?'.

b. There may be aspects of our teaching programme, particularly in the affective domain, which is is difficult, impossible or undesirable to assess. How do we evaluate our work in these areas?

c. The distinction between process and product assessment also contributes to a fuller picture of pupil achievement. For example, in a practical subject is there a value in assessing a pupil 'at work' or is it adequate to assess his 'finished article'?

How do we assess?

a. A variety of assessment techniques will probably be needed to cover adequately the range of objectives of any one department.

b. Formal tests, producing 'objective' scores will probably be required as part of the assessment procedure in most departments.

c. In areas where subjective marking predominates, strategies for moderation and standardisation will be required.

d. NORM-REFERENCED GRADES. Comparing a pupil's performance with others in the same year group is valued by parents and assist us in classifying pupils for setting or examination entry. In order to produce standardisation in the use of numbered grades for year group tests the following procedure has been agreed:

149

When tests or examinations are set across a whole year group, results on the new report system will be reported to parents using the numbered grade system. Grades 1–5 with 1 as the highest grade. These grades will give an indication of a pupil's performance in relation to a year group. At the same time it is undesirable that lower grades should be demotivating.

NFER test results suggest that Putteridge pupils do not conform to the national 'normal distribution curve'. As a result it would be a disservice to our pupils to distribute grades in line with this curve, which would give:

GRADE 1	2	3	4	5
10%	20%	40%	20%	10%

In doing this we may be encouraged to think in terms of a normal distribution, for example, in predicting examination success. There is a danger then of lowered expectation.

However we do need an element of standardisation across the school in our use of 'norm-referenced' grades. It is suggested that these grades should be distributed according to an agreed pattern.

To take account of the 'measured ability' of our pupils and to bear some relationship to the national level of performance it is suggested that grades should be awarded according to the following pattern:

For any population taking a 'norm-referenced' test:

GRADE 1	2	3	4	5
14%	32%	42%	10%	2%

This distribution is presented as a guide to departments. It is essential that there is an objective measure of standardisation, so it cannot be ignored! At the same time the distribution need not be RIGIDLY applied — helpful clues often emerge by graphing a set of results, revealing natural breaks in the mark distribution, etc.

e. CRITERION-REFERENCED GRADES. Measuring individual achievement against a pre-determined standard. Criterion-referenced grading does not attempt to create a rank order, nor to compare one pupil's performance with another. This style of assessment is not primarily aimed at discriminating between the performances of different pupils. It is possible that on a specific criterion-referenced assessment test all pupils may perform well and achieve the higher grades available.

Grades A, B, C and D are used for this style of assessment and, as the departmental contributions to the assessment booklet show, in many cases an agreed scale has been produced against which items of work may be graded.

These lettered grades are normally used with assessment items relating to one teaching group or set, assessing pupil achievement in relation to the work taught to that group.

Reports to parents will normally contain a combination of numbered (NR) grades and lettered (CR) grades.

In many cases the same test may be used for either NR or CR puproses — it is the way in which the results are used which primarily determines whether it is a NR or CR assessment.

'The essential difference is...that in one case the value we put on a pupil's performance depends on how it compares with a predefined standard while in the other case the value we attach depends on the performance of his fellow pupils.' (D Rowntree 1977)

f. Continuous, periodic or termly? Departments need to achieve a suitable balance in the timing and style of assessment procedures.

g. As pupils move through the school they need to encounter assessment techniques which will adequately prepare them for external examinations to be taken at the end of their courses.

Keeping records

1. Departments need to ensure that an adequate record-keeping system exists for each member of the department. The aims should be:

a. To provide accurate results and grades for transfer to report forms.

b. To have available up-to-date information about individual pupils' achievements.

c. To facilitate internal moderation of standards and statistical analysis — eg. compilation of results for norm-referenced grading.

2. *Records of achievement.* This is a cumulative record of personal achievements, kept by each child. It is intended to provide positive motivation and to increase pupils' awareness of the school's interest in their total development.

A folder for each child is stored in the Form Room and is accessible to the pupil. It can contain certificates of achievement in a variety of activities. A summary sheet contains details of all achievements, endorsed by staff signatures. The responsibility for updating rests with the pupil and it can contain an endless range of achievements. Examples might include:

— music examination awards

— sports certificates

— letters of commendation

— school certificates for attendance, punctuality

— activities records and certificates, eg. contributions to clubs, societies, etc

— achievements out of school, eg. sports, clubs, community service, etc

The folder will accumulate records over five years, contributing to our knowledge of a pupil when writing testimonials/references in year 5.

3. *Record of progress and attainment.* The main objectives behind this record are:

i. to inform form tutors about the progress of their pupils' work;

ii. to achieve this with the minimum of administration;

It is intended that the record should indicate:

1. The attainment of a pupil in relation to the range of learning opportunities offered to him or her in the subject during the appropriate term. Pupil attainment is not measured in comparison with other pupils,

and a term's work would be unlikely to produce a 'normal distribution' within a teaching group.

2. An overview of the pattern of progress across a variety of subjects, and across time. Subject teachers have the opportunity to indicate whether 'suitable progress is being made', or whether 'progress causes concern'.

The responsibility for monitoring the work progress of a pupil remains the primary responsibility of the departments. The form tutor, however, is offered information to facilitate the identification of trends and cross-subject concerns.

Reports and parents' evenings

The assessment booklet illustrates the variety of assessment methods being used by departments. Each departmental section indicates the categories which are used on report forms for communication of grades to parents. The report form for each department also allows for a comprehensive written comment. The written comment allows for communication in words about aspects of our assessment which are not adequately covered by the grading system:

a. A more subjective appraisal of pupil achievement... 'that which floats to the top of the teacher's awareness'. (Marshall 1968[1])

b. Aspects such as presentation of work, oral ability or attitude which may not be graded.

c. An expansion or summary of grade details.

d. Relevant social development relating to the work of the pupil.

e. Pleasing or disturbing aspects of the pupil's work.

f. Specific advice for action or improvement in the future.

g. A deliberate attempt to motivate by positive feedback to pupil and parent.

The parents' evening which follows each set of reports is an opportunity to complete the report by personal contact. An element of 'parent education' exists here, in aiding parents' understanding of the content and style of the report.

A fuller picture of the school's assessment policies, including departmental contributions, may be found in the school assessment booklet.

Summary — A profile of pupil achievement

It is recognised that no single method of assessment can produce a full picture of pupil achievement. Equally it is recognised that a system which segments aspects of achievement and performance into too many discrete parts can lack coherence and synthesis. The school's approach to producing a profile of achievement has three main dimensions:

a. DEPARTMENTAL ASSESSMENT PROCEDURES. This aspect offers a sophistication of technique and a range or parameters appropriate to

---

[1] Marshall M S (1968). *Teaching without Grades*. Corallis, Oregon: Oregon State University Press.

the assessment of a wide and varied curriculum. It includes objective measurement of pupil performance against a variety of criteria.

b. PROGRESS AND ATTAINMENT RECORDS. This element provides well informed subjective assessment of pupil performance. It allows teachers to summarise trends in pupil progress in a manageable and accessible form.

c. RECORDS OF ACHIEVEMENT. This element recognises that the individual being 'profiled' has a right to make a contribution. It is also possible in this record to take account of achievements which are not readily embraced within the classroom learning context.

These three elements of assessment contribute to a knowledge and understanding of a wide range of pupil achievements. However, it is essential at all times to remember that it is a view of the whole person which is required to assess the success of the education process. There is no substitute for the knowledge of persons derived from good personal human relationships.

We must not lose sight of the prime objective in evaluation and assessment: the improvement of teacher: pupil relationships in the school situation and an improvement in educational standards. It is too easy to concentrate upon the quality and detail of records, too attractive to segment continuously pupils like oranges, and to break skills down into meaningless detail. The quality of a profile is not to be judged by the thickness of a file or even the value to an employer, but by the success achieved in the build-up of knowledge of the pupil response to learning translated into improved teacher techniques and strategies and improved pupil performance. Do the teachers know more about the pupils and the ways in which they learn? Do the pupils learn more effectively? These should be the prime objectives of assessment and evaluation.

Acknowledgements

The past and continued development of the processes of assessment and evaluation in the school has been achieved by the endeavours of a professional and committed teaching Staff, past and present, supported by central and local professional agencies and colleagues who have advised, participated and monitored with enthusiasm and energy. The key to our success has been our dedication to educational principles translated into realistic aims and objectives, paced by related policies and co-ordinated strategies which essentially preserved the concept and actuality of whole school growth nurturing the involvement and welfare of everyone.

The Role and Responsibility of the Local Education Authority

4.1 Teacher Appraisal

Duncan G. Graham, County Education Officer, Suffolk

One of the more remarkable features of the English system has been how recently quite fundamental questions about relative responsibilities have been posed, let alone answered. When comparisons with more centralised systems are made, there is a defensiveness about how we justify the merits of sturdy independence and of 'vive. la difference'. While conformity is dull and undesirable, licence can be difficult to explain to public and parents. In more practical terms any kind of objective performance measurement tends in England to fall at the first hurdle — who is going to do it, and who has the power to be responsible for consistency?

In the last few years we have, under financial pressure and unease about the relevance of the curriculum, started to answer these questions. As a result the need for broad national criteria to be established has been accepted, the large measure of discretion which is, and ought to be, left to schools confirmed, and a more positive role for the LEA developed. In curriculum the combination of papers culminating in *Better Schools* exemplifies the national role, and LEA curricula established in response to Circular 6/81[1] their position which is to provide a local framework within which schools can operate, paying due regard to national criteria, but going far beyond them. Our Suffolk Curricular Papers, which include a separate explanatory document for the community, are I suppose typical of these.

Predating these developments in many LEAs were attempts to measure and monitor output or quality. This was not, I think, a crude response to cash constraints — a simple 'bang for the buck' reaction. More fundamentally it sprang from unease about questions which could not be answered, — and frankly a few bad schools and small numbers of bad teachers whom it was difficult to do much about: it is a sobering fact that some members of LEAs and administrators questioned whether it was even their right or duty to take remedial measures!

Fortunately there are today few, if any, LEAs which do not see establishing a curriculum as a main function — after consultation and discussion — and monitoring its implementation as a major part of its day-to-day work.

[1] *The School Curriculum*, DES 1981.

In Suffolk we took the view some years ago that four parts of our work were inextricably linked — curriculum development, in-service training with the emphasis on management, appraisal of schools and appraisal of teachers. For the purposes of this paper I shall concentrate on the last of these, but I must emphasise that only a policy which embraces all four will work. There is a particularly close relationship between school and teacher appraisal. Stuart Johnson's paper (see page 159) deals with the former. I would echo much of what he says. The major differences between our developments have been that Suffolk has tended to develop a school's ability for self-appraisal first, with a comprehensive scheme introduced in 1980, and sees school 'reviews' (note the semantics!) as complementary to them. We review some 18 schools each year. Warts and all, the system tends to assist schools materially, enables the authority to monitor progress and quality, and provides reassurance to parents and public. School appraisal, sensitively handled, is an instrument for effecting change and measuring performance: clearly, the more it is conducted by the school itself the better, but the wider context must be there.

What of teacher appraisal? As you will know research funded by the DES — earthy rather than academic — led to the publication in the summer of this year of *Those Having Torches*[1] (or 'tortures' as one journalist described it in a revealingly Freudian review!). I will not attempt to précis it, but will try to draw out the findings most relevant to our subject.

The arguments in principle are compelling. Teachers are the bedrock of the system, the rest of us mere infrastructure. We stand or fall by their classroom performance, their belief in the curriculum, their ability to assess their strengths and weaknesses, and to change and adapt from a basis of self-awareness. With a more structured curriculum, more rigorous review of school performance, and hopefully before long an agreed contractual concept of teachers' duties, only a history of failure elsewhere could deflect us from investing time, resource and effort to teacher appraisal. We found that teacher appraisal was not a panacea, but that provided certain ingredients were present, and certain pitfalls avoided, investment in it could reap a rich harvest — for teachers, and for the community. In short a valid scheme perceptibly improves performance and job-satisfaction. What are the criteria for success?

1. If it is to be widely acceptable and reassuring to the public, there must be national criteria which ensure consistency of application, a monitoring of standards between schools and LEAs, and, in time, a system where references based on appraisal have a national validity — which they certainly do

---

[1]Suffolk Education Department (1985). *Those Having Torches: Teacher Appraisal.* A study funded by the DES. Ipswich: the Education Department. (Title taken from Plato *Republic*: 'Those having torches will pass them on to others').

not have now. Simplistic criteria based on legislation would
not necessarily achieve this — there is nothing easier to
invalidate by indifference. Enabling legislation would be
preferable, provided that it enabled resource allocation as well.

2. The LEA must have a central role in establishing, monitoring
and supporting the scheme. The system will only work in
quality terms if it is 95 per cent institution-based, but the
other 5 per cent is vital. It involves 'quality control', training
of assessors, in-service support tailored to individual needs,
and more immediate involvement in the appraisal of heads,
advisers, and officers.

3. While there is scope for a fair degree of variation in practices
within LEAs and within schools, and this should be
encouraged, the common characteristics must be:

  i. The scheme must be negotiated openly and freely with
  teachers and their representatives.

  ii. It must be 'user-friendly': it must be introduced with good
  material and explanatory literature.

  iii. It must be based on partnership and trust between the
  appraiser and the appraised. It must therefore be formative
  and not summative.

  iv. The appraisers must be credible, highly trained and
  consistent.

  v. Classroom observation will be a vitally important
  component. Methodology for this does exist but needs
  development.

  vi. It needs to result in conclusions in each case which are
  honest and constructive, with the accent on personal development within the framework of the needs of the service.

  vii. As schools, in consultation with LEAs, need to set themselves better defined and clearer goals, so do teachers within
  their schools.

  viii. While there should be no immediate links between appraisal
  and salary, it should be recognised that there is a correlation
  between good appraisal performance and career advancement, and less good performance and questions being asked.
  More positive help for struggling teachers is long overdue.

  ix. As a consequence of appraisal, promotion procedures will
  have to be rethought. Appraisal gives opportunities for
  greater professional participation in appointments. It will
  give LEAs better opportunities for man-management, 'fast-
  tracking', and so on. How ironic it will be if pending legislation kicks into touch such an obvious prop to better quality, and one in the hands of managers in the private sector.

The next step is to flesh out within the framework the detailed roles of government, LEAs, Unions and schools, to formulate the training programmes — the first major package is now complete in Suffolk — and above all to get the KEY processes right. All the Barkises appear to be willing — we must hope that ESGs are operating soon and the essential preliminaries to implementation being overtaken.

One minor problem remains — the cost of teacher appraisal. This will be a revealing indicator of real commitment. The cost is significant and cannot be credibly fudged. If we hear that fatal and familiar phrase 'within existing resources' we should beware — there are too many vivid illustrations of the caricatures of schemes which come from insufficient resource commitment. There are 'new' costs in senior staff time, and the setting up of a permanent training scheme for evaluators, and responding to needs identified at appraisal would knock a nasty hole in most LEA INSET budgets; the paper work and administrative staff would not be negligible in cost, and LEA senior management would have to be strengthened to cope. At an estimated 12–15 man hours per assessment the overall impact on the system is appreciable.

I would wish to emphasise the importance of being able to analyse and define outcomes which are realistic and practicable and for which the resources are available for implementation at school and authority level. I trust there will be no conflict with proposals currently under consideration that could lessen individual authorities 'freedom to act' in the field of in-service education.

Before relating teacher-assessment to the overall support which an LEA should give its schools, it is worth looking for a moment at the role of the adviser in the process. It is in my view too easy to see a major role for them here *per se*. Their expertise, like that of HMI, is in curriculum management rather than in line management or personnel management. I predict that we will find that a new breed of animal will emerge — from the ranks of heads, advisers, teachers, officers — those with a particular expertise in an exacting craft, and that they will conduct assessment of senior staff, and supervise the wider process within schools and in partnership with heads. This will in no way diminish the role of advisers whose work is more appropriately, in my view, with curriculum development and school appraisal, in supporting the individual teacher outside the appraisal process and arising from it, and in acting as 'consultant' to appraisers. The complementary role of advisers and 'appraisers in chief' is obvious. The ultimate responsibility to committee for quality lies with the CEO. He will simply need more professional staff than he has now — belatedly it is being recognised that such staff are probably the most cost-effective we have.

Extending the best of present practice into the future, I should like to see a clearly stated national policy on the constituent parts of quality control — curriculum, staffing, appraisal, examinations, and so on. I should like to see more evidence that it is formulated after listening to the voice of local government practictioners, and that questions about consistency among and between government initiatives are being considered. That said, there must be enormous scope for LEAs to devise strategies of their own to satisfy criteria where they exist, and in local terms, and at the same time to support schools in areas where there are no national policies — and these should be many. LEAs should devise with their schools a curriculum policy which is clear, consistent and helpful, but leaves the maximum discretion with schools. Each LEA should support schools through its advisory service, and use advisers and officers, and members and governors too, to gather intelligence to help it identify and recognise good practice and eliminate bad practice. It should assist its schools to self-reliance on assessment and evaluation of performance, backed up by systematic reviews, and its teachers to higher performance by appraisal school-based, but LEA-administered. It must much more confidently identify and praise the good, and pinpoint and deal with the less good. To do that it must be confident of its own monitoring and intelligence-gathering systems, and its own ability to evaluate, and to lead from the front! In a defined curriculum, in school and teacher appraisal, in professionally strong advisers and officers it has the tools. All it needs is the will — and the resources.

The Role and Responsibility of the Local Education Authority

4.2 The Assessment of Schools

Stuart Johnson, CBE, Director of Education, Leeds

The opportunity to write a paper on ways in which we can make assessments of the effectiveness of schools in one which I welcome, though I am aware that I must enter an area which is seen to be fraught with difficulties, tensions and disagreements. I welcome that opportunity not because of any masochistic tendency on my part — though the capacity to withstand more than a little discomfort must, in present circumstances, be a necessary quality in all Chief Education Officers — but because it is a subject of endless interest and because we are now at a point in the development of our educational system when we can no longer afford to accept measures of school effectiveness which are not based on long and tested practice and which do not carry with them the confidence of all those taking part in such judgements. Too many assumptions are made by those who do not understand the complexities of managing schools and organising the curricula within them. Those assumptions are damaging to the development of new ideas and methods, the allocation of resources and to the very standing of education within the social framework itself. Unless we begin to demonstrate quite clearly, for all to see, that the coinage of education is not being debased, that the school systems we operate do represent real value for the time and effort, the research and study, the commitment and devotion, as much as for the financial expenditure made upon them, then we are unable properly to counter the charges of ineffectiveness.

I am optimistic about the process of making assessments of schools; I am optimistic about the possibility of developing criteria of assessment with a national validity; and I am optimistic about teachers being able to accept processes and strategies which allow the objective assessment of schools and which do not offend those whose work is being subjected to that assessment. There is enough experience of helping schools and teachers within my own Authority to give me that optimism, and the evidence is hard enough and well-documented enough to allow me to base my case upon it.

The HMI study of school evaluation 'Quality in Schools — Evaluation and Appraisal' acknowledges the inconsistency of use of terms such as appraisal, review, evaluation and assessment. The distinctions that one

---

[1]DES. *Quality in Schools: Evaluation and Appraisal.* An HMI study. HMSO, 1985.

can make between such terms are very often narrow and confusing. I have chosen to use the term 'assessment' in speaking of the process of measuring the degree of success a school may be achieving. I choose 'assessment' because it carries no semantic overtones of praise or blame; it does not have the pomposity of a term such as 'judgement', nor does it touch the raw nerve exposed by 'inspection'. The objectivity, the broad perspective, the concern for the whole range of objectives within a school as an institution in its own right and as part of the community to which it belongs are caught up into the term so that, in 'assessing' a school we are making a careful observation and analysis, distinguishing the base from the precious metal, determining the nature of the amalgam, with the visitors acting as informed consultants.

The ideal to which I work is that of a 'co-operative assessment' in which there is a mutual responsibility for all parties to be open, frank, generous in their analysis and, above all, positive in the conclusions which they reach and clear in their indication of future action. I look towards a situation in which 'assessors' and 'assessed' are genuinely indistinguishable from each other. In the fullness of time the assessors and the assessed are, in absolute fact, the same people, as teachers acquire the objectivity, the vision, the confidence and the humility to be able to make assessment of their own work against local authority and national standards.

School-assessment issues

Let me now examine some of the issues to be faced in assessing a school's achievements. Some, of course, I have hinted at already. These issues include establishing a clear programme of assessments within an authority, ensuring that a broad spectrum of schools is involved so that there can be no belief that only failing schools are assessed, or that schools in particular areas of the authority are more likely to be assessed. Thus a fair and complete picture of the whole authority is drawn and bench marks are set for use by all schools and advisers in their own assessments. A good deal of training and preparation needs to be done within that section of an authority's Department of Education which is, initially, responsible for leading an assessment. Under normal circumstances the responsibility clearly lies with the advisers or inspectors of the authority, though other divisions of the Department have much to offer to the process of assessment and their involvement is often crucial. The drawing-up of a guideline document to direct the progress of an assessment is crucial and that document, which is made available to all schools, should be regularly reviewed. Decisions need to be taken about the size of teams to be involved, to whom the assessment will be reported, how recommendations resulting from the assessment are acted upon. Preparation for and the anticipation of possible hindrances and obstacles are issues which cannot be ignored. They are critical to the success of the whole enterprise.

Nothing should come to the school involved as a surprise. Co-operation between assessors and assessed is vital. If it is possible to give a school options as to the time and length of an assessment — or indeed whether the assessment is to be made at all — then those options must be given. A great deal depends upon the relationship developed between teachers and officers in this respect. How easily a school assessment can begin will indicate the quality of the work of an authority's advisorate, of the confidence advisers are able to engender in teachers who, in spite of all assurances to the contrary, will inevitably feel threatened. A clear indication of procedures to be followed and a time-scale which allows for discussion in the school and for adjustment to an interruption of the school's basic routine are thus vital. Adherence to the procedure is important too, though it is accepted that understaffing in schools and in the advisorate, sudden disruptions of the anticipated programme of work and unexpected difficulties will all play a part in delaying the completion of the exercise. I do not advocate a rigid adherence; local circumstances will require a modification of procedure but, from the outset, every attempt must be made to allow schools to act as equal partners in making decisions, to understand what is happening and what they can anticipate.

I believe that co-operation is of the essence in such enterprises as this and regular opportunities to discuss their progress are provided. The communication systems set up are as short, as direct and as all-embracing as can be devised.

The ultimate aim of an assessment is to build oppotunities for future self-assessment and an efficient advisorate will, in its management and curricular training programmes, have evolved the criteria by which school effectiveness can be assessed and will have communicated these criteria broadly through the authority. During the progress of the assessment, fostering self-analysis and urging teachers to set out their own apprehension of how the systems and methods they have established are working, those criteria will be put into operation.

It is important, too, that everyone involved in the assessment has access to a suitably detailed database. The compilation of that database is not a light undertaking to be done hastily during the process of the exercise. It is an important part of the strategy. I advocate that the preparation for the assessment includes the compilation of data which gives a clear picture not only of a school's staffing, curriculum and resources, but also of its aims and objectives and of the context in which the school operates. However carefully the work of a school may be geared to the policies of the authority, to the recommendations of the various reports of HM Inspectorate or to the

161

demands of a regional examinations board, much of its work may be
wasted if it lacks relevance to the situations in which it locally
operates. Parental expectations and support, the level of staffing and
resources (both quantitatively and qualitatively), the ethos of the
school, the philosophies which have dictated the aims and objectives
which it has established, and the present and anticipated movements
in the size of the school's roll are important considerations which it is
foolhardy to ignore.

The headteacher's key role

In terms of the assessment of a school as much as of the appraisal of
teachers the central importance of the role of the headteacher must be
acknowledged, whether the school be a tiny country school or a large
urban comprehensive school with a sophisticated management
structure and a wide range of subject disciplines within its curriculum.
In assessing a school we are, perhaps above all else, assessing the
foresight, the imagination, the competence in managerial as much as
in curricular terms and the resourcefulness of the headteacher. All the
work that has been done in my Authority, whether on the co-operative
assessment of schools, on the developmental self-analysis to which we
hope schools will move or on the National Development Council's
management project in which Leeds is actively involved, underlines
the need for the active participation of the headteacher. These are
responsibilities which cannot be delegated — though other teachers
may be involved — because they touch on the motivation and
organisation of forward momentum in the school. It is my view that in
the assessment of schools, through the headteacher and through the
staff of those schools, lies a new and deeply significant motivation to
the development and enhancement of the ways in which we educate
our children — towards better schools.

Assessment based on a consideration of the issues I have described in
some detail offer an opportunity for the operation of individual schools
to be analysed, carefully and in a manner which does not threaten
those who feel they are failing — and there are many teachers who,
quite wrongly, have a feeling of failure — and those who know they
are failing but flinch from admitting it. Such assessments allow those
teachers to take up new stances and even to make new beginnings,
which will give greater confidence and present opportunities for
grasping the exciting new initiatives that are there for all of us. I do
not exclude from this opportunity either advisers or administrators.
The diffusion of good practice across an authority and thence across
the nation is a central part of the work of authority officers and of
HMIs.

'Co-operative assessments' of Leeds schools

It is against a background of thinking such as this that, in Leeds, over
the past eight years we have sought to develop a pattern of what I

have chosen to call 'co-operative assessments' of schools. We have spent time and thought in refining the system and feel not a little pleased that we have been able to anticipate a trend which has grown in strength and volume over more recent years. We choose to call our assessments 'consultative visits', being conscious of the importance of finding a title which will remove any sense of a traditional type of inspection. All that is done is based on a patterned procedure set out in a guideline document which is available to any of the Authority's 400 schools on request. The Department's Management Group — the Education Officer's Group — approves an annual programme on which limitations must be placed by the availability of advisory staff. A programme aims at visiting three primary schools, one middle school and one high school in each academic year, with a visit to a special school or to a college of further education in alternate years. Attempts are made to ensure that each year's programme is a cross-section of the Authority's provision. Schools from each of the five administrative areas of Leeds are included, some which have inner-urban catchments and others from the semi-rural and small market town catchments in the Authority. The temptation to concentrate the efforts of limited and decreasing manpower only on those schools where there seems to be greatest need of development is set aside.

Absolute confidentiality is maintained between the schools involved and the officers of the Authority. This confidentiality has done much to persuade schools that in helping to assess their own performance they do not risk exposure to either ridicule or disdain. The ultimate goal towards which we work is that schools themselves will request involvement in a consultative visit because they feel that the visit allows them to draw up a plan of future action, covering five or ten years, with well-defined stages of development, specific aims and objectives and a clear understanding of future trends.

The procedures followed are then very straightforward. The chief adviser and the adviser with pastoral responsibility for the school nominated by the Department's management team visit the school, speak with the headteacher and seek the co-operation of the school in the exercise. If it is refused — and there may be many reasons why a school could, with perfect propriety, refuse involvement — then at that point the matter ends for the time being. In fact, in eight years, no school has refused, though adjustments have been made to find dates for the visit which suit the school's calendar better than those originally suggested. The wise headteacher, however willing to become involved, seeks the co-operation and approval of the staff before committing the school, and I require the assurance that this has been done before we proceed with a visit.

Any outstanding difficulties, apprehensions and concerns can be removed at the next stage of the exercise. If an approval to proceed, however conditional, is given, then the senior adviser for the tier of

163

schooling to which the school belongs visits the school with the general adviser and gives a detailed account of the programme anticipated, making adjustments and modifications to suit the needs of the school and the staff and, hopefully, fixing the dates and parameters of assessment. The Authority does not have directive documentation in respect of curriculum, though there are extensive guidelines and the Chairman of the Education Committee has set out the ways in which he hopes curriculum will develop in the Authority. Nor is there documentation which would act as an infallible check-list of a school's efficiency: there are too many variables involved. The parameters of which I speak are those which indicate the functions of the school which will be subject to the assessment. In the vast majority of cases the whole range of the school's work will be discussed, leaving nothing out. If, however, a school is encountering special difficulties because of staffing problems in one area of the curriculum, then there may be discussion about how that area may be treated during the visit.

In this field the value and importance of documents such as *Better Schools* and *The Curriculum from 5 to 16* are paramount. The presentation of a national framework of objectives for education and a clear delineation of the parameters by which assessment can be made will clarify the main goals towards which schools should move, though allowing for differences in emphasis and balance reflecting local circumstances and local judgements. I believe that the proposition that the curriculum of every school should have breadth, balance, relevance and differentiation is a classically economical definition of what the best of our schools have always sought to provide, and that within that proposition and its refinement through the definitions offered within *Better Schools* lies the key checklist by which a school can now assess its performance.

Between this meeting with the school and the beginning of the visit there is much to be done. The general adviser for the school, who becomes responsible for co-ordinating the logistics of the visit, collects the background documentation to the school's operation. The great bulk is available from the school itself and the immediacy of the availability of documentation is a measure of a school's efficiency and preparedness. Other material can be gathered from the various divisions of the Education Department and from agencies to which the school may have had recourse. The good general adviser will know what materials are needed for consultative visits and will, with the school, have prepared many documents well in advance. The general adviser aims to assemble enough material to give a detailed picture of the school's location and catchment, probable movements in its roll, details of staffing resources (both material and financial) and attendance records within the school. Anything that assists in giving a clear picture of the school and the contexts in which it is operating is included. Familiarity with this material prevents false judgements being made and speeds the process of the assessment by allowing more time to be spent on present facts and discussion of the future rather than an analysis of the past.

Meanwhile the senior adviser leading the exercise will have drawn together and will have apprised the headteacher of the team to visit the school. The chief adviser builds a team carefully, in consultation with colleagues, to make sure there is a blend of those who know the school well and those less familiar with it and therefore likely to be able to bring a fresh perspective to the view. The size of the team, and its composition, will depend upon the designation and size of the school or college visited. A small primary school needs no more than a small team of six general advisers, some with specialist primary experience, others with special subject skills. A middle school, of which Leeds has 65, requires a larger team because of the subject specialisms which will be discussed: perhaps 12 advisers for a four-form entry school. One of the Authority's 50 high schools requires a full team of 17 or 18 members so that all subject specialisms, however detailed and advanced their work, can be covered. Not all members of the team will be in the school simultaneously — the general adviser for the school has the task of co-ordinating the presence of advisers so that, during the visit, every teacher has the chance to be seen in the classroom working with pupils, time to talk to advisers and time to discuss what will be the substance of the observations made in any report which will be written. If the visit is well co-ordinated, then there will be no disruption of the normal pattern of the school's operation and minimal interruption of teachers' and pupils' timetables. Advisers make every effort to integrate themselves into the life of the school and are as much interested in its extra-curricular work as in its curricular and pastoral operation.

The senior adviser's presence in the school will be more frequent than that of colleagues. The greater part of that officer's work will be with the Head Teacher and the senior managers, with the secretarial staff and with the caretaker, with ancillary staff and the staff of agencies such as libraries and detached centres, sports centres and youth clubs. Each day of the visit should, ideally, be concluded by a discussion between the headteacher and the senior adviser on the day's work and on the progress of the visit. Difficulties can thus be resolved with a minimum of delay. Regular discussions between teachers and members of the advisory team are vital. No teacher should be visited in class without prior arrangement and ample time should be given for preparation and discussion. Nothing should come as an unwelcome surprise to the headteacher or to staff and the establishment of a positive and supportive relationship between teachers and officers is regarded as being of paramount importance.

Sustaining the effort of the visit can be taxing and for this reason visits are kept as short as possible. A visit to a primary or special school is generally accomplished within a working week. A middle

school or high school because of its size and complexity takes longer
— as much as three weeks in the case of a large high school.

The report-writing stage

At the end of the visit the senior adviser spends some time setting out
to the headteacher the team's initial impressions. No individual
teacher will be named and as positive a note as possible will be struck.
What is said by the senior adviser at this stage will directly guide what
will be written in the report submitted by officers to the school at the
earliest opportunity. Let me be frank and say that it is the report-
writing stage which has thrown up difficulties, not of acceptance or
interpretation but of logistics and delay caused by the pressure of
other business which, however transient may have been the issues, had
allowed no delay.

The report produced, which is to the school and to the Education
Officers' Group that commissioned the visit, is regarded as extremely
confidential. Members of the Advisory Division not involved in the
visit do not have free access to the report which is written by the
senior adviser leading the team, though general lessons to be learned
from visits are discussed in the Advisory Division. It is backed up by
an appendix of individual subject reports written to a strict pattern.
Standardisation of reporting is seen as being very important and each
report covers the following areas: the environment of the school and
its effect upon the work of the school; the school buildings; the
curriculum; staffing and management; ethos and philosophy; in-service
training; resources; records; relationships with other agencies. Specific
issues such as links with the community, continuity of curriculum with
other tiers of education can be examined as separate elements of the
report if it is felt to be valuable. The subject reports cover items such
as aims and objectives, buildings and resources, documentation and
staffing, and end with clearly enunciated recommendations, all of
which will have been indicated to subject teachers and to the
headteacher. Again, nothing should come as a surprise.

When completed, the draft report, approved by the chief adviser, is
submitted to the headteacher for the correction of any errors of FACT.
Opinions and recommendations cannot be modified at this stage but it
would be wrong for errors of fact to be included. Generally there are
few such errors and these not in significant areas or dimensions. The
corrected second draft is sent for the approval of the management
team of the Department who indicate any modifications they may wish
to make and that draft is then published to the school. Two copies are
despatched, one printed on one side of the page only so that, if the
headteacher wishes, any of the subject reports can be issued privately
to the staff of that department. Whether the main body of the report
is issued to the staff of the school is for the headteacher to decide —
though in my opinion it would be foolish for a headteacher not to do

so. When the staff of the school has had time to digest the report there is a final visit made by the chief adviser, the senior adviser leading the team, the general adviser for the school and other advisers having taken part in the visit to discuss, in open forum, issues raised by the report and its recommendations.

Two more tasks remain. The main report, with the appendix of subject reports summarised, for these are often technical in nature, is submitted to the school's governing body. Finally, the work of the school is monitored over the 12 months succeeding the report and at the end of that period another round of discussions takes place, assessing again the strengths and weaknesses of the schools analysed by school and advisers. Modifications made as a result of the recommendations agreed in the report are noted.

Additional modifications of this basic pattern are always possible and special circumstances will inevitably indicate the special emphases which need to be placed on particular elements within the basic programme. Exercises have been undertaken which have allowed the Advisory Division of the Authority to work with a school over the whole of an academic year. This is expensive of advisory time and only to be undertaken after careful planning of the frequency of visiting. Such a visit is revealing of the intricacies of the work of schools and the complexity of the inter-relationships within them, between staff and pupils, pupils and their peers and between staff, pupils, parents. Another variation has been a programme which examined specific elements of a high school programme. This, a much shorter exercise, gave special insights into the ways in which that school anticipated its problems, analysed its annual intake and made special provision for those suffering from the disadvantages associated with unsupportive home backgrounds, poor language and number competence and alienation from schooling. I would also point to exercises which have involved consultants from higher education — a survey of a school's management structure — and colleagues from teacher education — the analysis of a high school's pastoral and tutorial system. In these ways advisers have a unique opportunity to see schools in all their seasons.

Assessment realism

This is not a perfect world. Resources are not always available to match the recommendations of such a report; staff changes leave holes in curriculum coverage; in-service training does not always produce the improvements and initiatives hoped for. An assessment honestly made and the recommendations and plans generated by such an assessment must accept that everything cannot be achieved immediately. Perhaps the real benefits which accrue from this sort of assessment lie in the discussion which takes place, the bonds which are made, the perspectives formed of future development, the motivation and excitement generated in an establishment perhaps fearful of change and in the broad improvements in attitude and spirit which accrue. Perhaps the medium is more important than the message.

Detailed work of this sort is of enormous value to the school which has taken part in the consultative visit. There is value to other schools in that lessons learned, techniques evolved and solutions found have relevance broadly across the Authority. But is this sufficient? Should not all schools have access to the programme within a reasonable period of time? There are nearly 400 schools and colleges in the Authority and the Advisory Service's time and manpower is not infinite. While maintaining a 'core' programme of consultative visits are there other possibilities for schools to gain a similar detailed assessment of their operation?

Self-assessment: a way forward

One way forward therefore lies in the development of self-assessment techniques within our schools. Against a background of study, consultation and discussion, the Authority has set out its philosophies in two documents. The first, *Looking at the Curriculum in Schools*[1], stresses the importance of staff consultation, of the drawing-up of guideline documentation, of the key role of the headteacher, of the influence of outside agencies and of recognising local contexts. The second document *Goals and Priorities for Education in Leeds*[2] points to the fundamental task of facing the changes occurring in society, in our cultural background and in our own expectations of work and leisure. Education needs to evolve more sensitive powers of identifying issues and of responding to them quickly and perceptively. A willingness to assess the state and effectiveness of the programmes offered by schools and for the schools to initiate and manage necessary change is, therefore, critical.

The Authority has produced curriculum guideline documentation which is backed up by curriculum position statements for the Education Committee. Each school is urged to produce its own staff development policy using the skills of trained staff tutors. A detailed in-service training programme completes the range of provision which has sought to encourage schools in Leeds to accept the ideas underlying assessment.

As a result of work already done in the Authority, Leeds was invited to take part in the project known as the Guidelines for Review and Internal Development in Schools (GRIDS) pilot scheme, which offers opportunity for involvement in a type of school evaluation that seeks to formalise a framework onto which can be built many of the good practices already identified in other exercises. It was decided to

[1,2] Copies of these documents are generally available from the Chief Adviser, Leeds City Council Department of Education, Merrion House, 110 Merrion Centre, Leeds LS2 8DT.

concentrate this project in a single administrative area of the Authority and to invite to take part a group of schools which were either involved in assessment processes, or were well-prepared to start such an experiment. The territorial unity aids inter-communication between schools and provides a homogeneity of backgrounds of the schools involved in the project. Status was given to the project by involving a team of advisers, all with a pastoral responsibility in the schools, a senior adviser and the Director of the Teachers' Centre. Evaluation and additional expertise have been provided by the University of Leeds, Leeds Polytechnic and a local College of Education.

Review and development by the school of the school are the key issues in this project and the energy and commitment shown in the trialling of the project have been remarkable. Working relationships between schools and within schools have been excellent; in-service training needs have been quickly identified and consultants from outside the school have been drawn in to supplement skills already in the schools.

So successful was the pilot project that it has now been extended to all schools wishing to take part and steering groups will be established in all five sectors of the City. The specific areas now being investigated include reviews by departments and specialist groups, identifying good practice, reviewing special educational needs and involving parents and governors.

GRIDS seek to devise a system which facilitates review by a school of what that school provides: an assessment of its effectiveness and the determination of ways and means of reaching the goals determined within the school as a result of that assessment. It emphasises democratic decision-making, encourages staff development and in-service training strategies within the school and demands that we look critically at ourselves so that we can seek to act upon the solutions to our problems. In doing these things GRIDS provides the next step forward from the consultative visit which I defined as the assessment of provision as a co-operative venture involving school and advisorate.

Our most recent involvement is that in the National Development Centre's project on management development based at Bristol. Again a small group of schools is involved, comprehending all four tiers of education, high, middle, primary and special. Again, a strong team from the advisorate is closely linked with the schools in their planning and discussion, and again the emphasis is on review, assessment and planning for development. The focus of study is the way in which we can train managers and develop management skills at all levels. Two areas are being specifically reviewed —the training of deputy head teachers and the training programmes and policies within the Department of Education itself. The exercise is valuable in demonstrating the ways in which headteachers can involve their staffs in the review of their domestic situations within the school. The work has confirmed the validity of the GRIDS process.

I began by saying that I am optimistic about the assessment of schools and I have put before you the evidence on which that optimism is based. Schools can and do co-operate in the detailed assessment of their work and this is achieved without any sense of insecurity or threat within the school. It is possible to review, to assess, to define aims and objectives, plan ways of achieving them and monitor progress towards those goals. It is possible to tap the springs of initiative and creativity which exist in our teaching staff once the conviction exists that there is genuine purpose in seeking new answers to old problems. And it is possible to do these things in a variety of ways as I have tried to show. If we are genuinely looking for better schools, then first we must assess their present position and we must do it sensitively and accurately. We must sift the good from the bad, using what has proved to be of value to guide us in designing policies and methods which will be the answers to the questions deriving from each school's unique experience.

The work of the past eight years in my Authority has indicated that in the consultative processes we have evolved, in the self-assessment strategies we have encouraged, in the staff development programme we have generously funded and in the optimistic view we have always sought to take of the future of education lies a positive way forward. By carefully assessing our present position, by realising strengths and weaknesses and by planning towards both local and national objectives, that way forward is made the easier, offering us both guidance and support.

APPENDIX

CONSULTATIVE VISITS

The purpose of consultative visits

Consultative visits are part of the Authority's arrangements for monitoring the education service. They are carried out jointly by the Advisory Service and the staff of the school or college concerned and are intended to assist the development of self-assessment procedures and skills, to provide working documents which can be used as guides to future development and, as appropriate, to provide general information helpful to the Authority in the formulation of its policies.

Each year's programme of visits includes a variety of types of schools and colleges, is representative of all geographical areas of the Authority, and attempts to reflect themes of current interest.

PRELIMINARY VISITS

1. An invitation to participate in a visit is delivered personally to the headteacher/ principal by the chief adviser and the general adviser for the school or college. It is explained precisely what a consultative visit is and what are its implications.

2. The invitation is followed shortly after by a meeting between all or representative staff and the chief adviser, the general adviser and the senior adviser who will be leading the visit. At this meeting the invitation is repeated, the purpose of the visit is explained, and an opportunity is provided for discussion and questions. If the invitation is accepted precise dates are agreed and the terms of the visit are then confirmed to writing by the Director of Education.

3. Before the formal visit begins the advisers taking part visit the school or college informally to meet members of staff. The general adviser collates documentary information to be given to all advisers taking part, and the senior adviser leading the visit agrees detailed arrangements for the visit with the headteacher or principal.

MEMBERSHIP OF THE ADVISORY TEAM

A consultative visit team is usually led by the senior adviser for the appropriate stage of education and always includes the general adviser for the school or college. As far as possible all areas of the curriculum are covered by members of the advisory team. In the case of small schools, in order to avoid the team being too large for the school to absorb, some areas of the curriculum may be covered by advisers who are not members of the consultative visit team and who will arrange mutually convenient single visits outside the period of the consultative visit. In all cases advisory membership of consultative visit teams is determined by the chief adviser in consultation with the senior adviser and general adviser concerned. It is the responsibility of the general adviser to draw to the attention of the senior adviser leading the team any need for specialist advisers to make short visits.

PRELIMINARY COLLECTION OF INFORMATION

1. The general adviser, in conjunction with the headteacher/principal, is responsible for gathering and collating information which is circulated only to other advisory members of the consultative visit team. The necessary information may be acquired by:

   a. reference to existing documentation held in the central Education Department, eg. form 7, school and college establishment sheets, etc;

   b. documentation available from the school or college;

   c. discussion and observation within the school or college.

2. The information may be arranged under the following headings:

   a. Location:
      i. the neighbourhood, noting any special social problems;
      ii. the feeder/receiving schools;
      iii. relevant demographic factors: catchment areas, division into ethnic or religious sub-groups;
      iv. site in relation to neighbourhood, transport, any particular difficulties;
      v. plan of buildings and campus, noting any special features, whether advantageous or disadvantageous, and any limitations imposed by the buildings or campus on organisation.

b. Features of School:

   i. ETHOS AND ASPIRATIONS:

     a. aims and objectives;

     b. prognosis of future development;

     c. any public statements such as handbooks.

   ii. TYPE AND HISTORY of development including reference to any organisational change and effects on staff recruitment, training and deployment.

   iii. SIZE:

     a. number of pupils/students including future projections of numbers;

     b. age range;

     c. class/group divisions;

     d. range of subjects, options, areas of curriculum or courses;

     e. staff list including indications of qualifications, training and responsibilities.

   iv. ORGANISATIONAL STRUCTURE

     a. management structures: job definition of senior staff;

     b. school/departmental lists of staff with indication of graded post allocations; staff movement;

     c. curriculum notation: allocation of times to subjects, option systems, setting/non-streamed teaching;

     d. systems of record-keeping;

     e. secretarial and ancillary staff: job descriptions of office and ancillary personnel, including bursars, clerical assistants, technicians, nursery nurses, teaching assistants and any other non-teaching staff;

     f. maintenance of school/college fabric;

     g. finances: money and equipment provided during the current year and the preceding five years from:

       1. LEA

         i. capitation;

         ii. capital loan;

         iii. other LEA source(s);

       2. sources other than LEA

         i. school/college fund;

         ii. PTA;

         iii. other source(s);

       3. allocation of financial resources and equipment;

       4. method of compiling and maintaining an inventory of stock and monitoring allocations of funds;

     h. code of discipline and types of sanction imposed, routines for pastoral periods and consultation, arrangements for monitoring attendance, rules and/or codes of behaviour and dress;

     i. travel/transport regulations and supervision, any special transport provision for purposes such as journeys to and from playing fields or baths, mini-bus transport, etc;

     j. daily/weekly/occasional routines such as registration and assembly procedures, fire and accident drills;

     k. supervision of movement within the building, security, arrangements for private study;

     l. links with home;

     m. links with the community including local industry;

     n. links between schools and colleges of further education.

  v. DOCUMENTATION

     a. methods of disseminating relevant information to staff, pupils/students and parents;

     b. policy statements on cross curricular areas such as language and careers education.

 vi. COMMUNICATION AND CONSULTATION

Arrangements for:

     a. decision-making;

     b. staff consultation;

     c. role and duty definitions and descriptions;

     d. links with parents;

     e. pupil/student participation in policy and decision-making;

     f. communication with the community and the governing body;

THE VISIT

1. Buildings

    a. How adequate are the facilities?

    b. To what extent is available space being used to the best advantage?

    c. What is the condition of the buildings?

    d. To what extent does everyone using the buildings contribute to the care of the fabric and environment?

    e. How far has the environment been made conducive to learning?

    f. To what extent is there a real sense of community and an atmosphere of mutual care and respect?

2. Policy and organisation

    a. How does the expressed educational policy work out in practice?

    b. To what extent are the policies, frameworks or schemes of work adequate to set appropriate short-term objectives and to ensure the overall development of concepts and skills?

    c. What evidence is there that the aims and objectives are known, understood and accepted by members of the school or college?

    d. What strategies are used to ensure parental involvement and how effective are the strategies in practice?

3. *Pupils/Students*

  a. How do the declared aims and objectives reflect the needs of the community served?

  b. To what extent is an appropriate and balanced educational programme provided for everyone?

  c. How far are members of staff aware of the background and need of individual pupils and students and how far does this awareness affect teaching approaches and organisation?

  d. What provision has been made for those with special needs, eg. slow learners, disadvantaged, gifted?

  e. What evidence is there that the aims and objectives are being realised in terms of pupils'/students' progress? Is there evidence of:

   i. the development of an understanding of the nature of the technological and multi-cultural character of contemporary society?

   ii. the development of positive attitudes to people, healthy living, work?

   iii. the development of necessary skills and concepts, (eg. language, mathematics, science, personal and social development, physical development and aesthetic development)?

   iv. successful performance as measured by any appropriate external assessment?

4. *Staff development*

  a. To what extent is the deployment of staff the optimum pattern to suit the needs of the school/college?

  b. To what extent is the potential of staff being fully used?

  c. How clear a view have staff of their roles?

  d. How effectively do staff interpret their roles in action?

  e. How effectively are non-teaching staff deployed?

5. *Staff Development and In-service Education*

  a. What is the policy of the school/college on release and support of staff for in-service education?

  b. Who decides who may apply for attendance at courses?

  c. How is information about in-service activities communicated to staff;

   i. before the activity takes place; and

   ii. after it has taken place?

  d. Is there a staff development policy? How does the headteacher/principal discover the career aspirations of staff and where possible help them to prepare for future promotion and professional development?

  e. What school-based or college-based or focussed programmes, if any, have been arranged in the last five years?

   f. What arrangements are made to look after students on teaching practice?

   g. What arrangements, if any, are made to induct probationary teachers and other new staff?

   h. What responsibilities for in-service education are carried by senior members of staff?

6. *Communication and Consultation*

   a. What are the professional relationships between:

      i. Headteacher/principal and senior staff?

      ii. Headteacher/principal and other teaching and non-teaching members of staff?

      iii. Members of staff and each other?

      iv. Pupils/students and the headteacher/principal, members of staff, other pupils/students?

   b. What are the methods of communication and to what extent are they satisfactory?

   c. To what extent do members of staff recognise and use each other's expertise?

7. *External Relations*

To what extent have appropriate and effective contacts been made with:

   a. establishments in the same and adjacent tiers of education?

   b. Governing or managing body?

   c. Careers Service?

   d. Continuing Education Service?

   e. Department of Social Service?

   f. Education Catering Service?

   g. Education Welfare Service?

   h. School Medical Service?

   i. Police liaison officers?

   j. Education Psychology Service?

8. *Specialist Subjects or Areas*

Specialist subjects or areas of the curriculum should be appraised with special reference to:

   a. area/departmental buildings and resources;

   b. staffing structures and timetables;

   c. organisation;

   d. communication;

   e. documentation;

f. ethos, ie. relationship within departments or groups and with external agencies such as other schools or colleges, support services, local businesses and industries, attempts to develop in pupils and students a sense of responsibility, freedom and involvement.

REPORTING

1. Throughout the visit advisers taking part frequently meet together and with teaching staff, as appropriate, to exchange and check information and to report progress. They discuss with the teachers with whom they are working the points to be made in the final report and the terms in which the report will be written. They have similar discussions with appropriate senior staff such as heads of department and year group leaders. Following these discussions a draft report will be prepared.

2. The senior adviser and the team taking part meet at the end of the visit to agree the general terms of the report which is a strictly confidential document.

3. Each member of the visiting team prepares a succinct report for presentation to the senior adviser concerned within two weeks of the end of the visit.

4. The senior adviser, after holding appropriate meetings with members of the team and teaching staff, provides a draft combined report for the chief adviser within eight weeks of the end of the visit.

5. The chief adviser discusses the document with the senior adviser and the visiting team and edits the final draft. This draft report is delivered by the general adviser to the headteacher or principal for discussion with senior staff and with the chief adviser and general adviser within the next few days. Any necessary amendments are then made and any divergent views of the school or college are recorded in the report.

6. The report is then presented to the Director of Education and his Departmental senior management team for comment which is incorporated in the report as necessary.

7. The report is then delivered to the headteacher or principal and arrangements made for the chief adviser, senior adviser and general adviser to meet all the staff to discuss the report.

8. A shortened version of the report will be prepared by the chief adviser for presentation to the managing/governing body.

IT IS EMPHASISED THROUGHOUT THAT CONSULTATIVE VISIT REPORTS ARE STRICTLY CONFIDENTIAL

FOLLOW-UP

1. The report should be considered as a working and development document for teachers and advisers, and supplementary visits will be made by appropriate advisers.

2. About a year after the visit the senior adviser who led the team and the general adviser visit the school or college to review with the headteacher or principal, and other staff as agreed, the progress made since the initial presentation of the report.

3. Further follow-up procedures are agreed with the school or college.

4. Throughout the exercise assistance is given to the school or college to develop its own self-appraisal procedures.

5. The leader of the team is responsible for keeping a reference copy of the report of the visit for the Advisory Division.

Acknowledgements

Thanks are due to Mr John West, Acting Chief Adviser, Leeds Department of Education, and Miss Brenda Howe, formerly Chief Adviser, who kindly read and passed comments on this paper.

The Role and Responsibility of the Secretary of State

*Speech by the Rt Hon Sir Keith Joseph, Bt, MP,
Secretary of State for Education and Science*

The proposals that I made in my speech to the North of England Conference[1] nearly two years ago were very widely welcomed. That was so, I believe, both because they were in tune with a great deal of work going on in schools and LEAs throughout the country, and because they expressed the shared objectives of the education service for improving the education offered to our young people.

The holder of my office is in a unique position to articulate those shared objectives. I shall today be speaking largely about measures that can be undertaken only from the centre, about the responsibilities that the holder of my office has to exercise. But I should like it to be quite clear that the fundamental purpose of everything that I shall mention is to help to improve what goes on in the classroom. My part is to promote a variety of measures directed to that end, while preserving — indeed taking advantage of — the flexibility of our education system. That is the background against which the Government's policies for education — set out most fully in *Better Schools* — should be seen.

Better Schools therefore set out not only our programme for change — *how* we proposed to achieve certain results, but also the Government's philosophy — *why* we wish to achieve these results. It contained many specific proposals for action, covering a wide range of topics: the curriculum; examinations; teaching approaches, teacher training and teacher management; and school government — to name only the larger areas. Together these proposals constitute a far-reaching programme for improving the performance of our schools.

The implementation of this programme will require a range of what one might broadly term 'administrative' action: legislation, regulations, the approval of teacher training courses, the establishment of new examination syllabuses, and so on.

Much of the action at this level will entail careful discussion of complex and difficult issues between the partners in the education

---

[1] Speech by the Rt Hon Sir Keith Joseph, Secretary of State for Education and Science, at The North of England Education Conference, Sheffield, on Friday 6 January 1984. (DES. Press Notice 1/84). See also *Oxford Review of Education* vol 10, No 2, February 1984. Abingdon (Oxon.): Carfax Publishing Company.

service. But, generally speaking, it will not be too difficult at that level to monitor progress, as we shall need to do.

I propose to concentrate rather on the considerably more intricate problems which arise at another level and with which many of the papers at this conference have been concerned. The 'administrative' level of action relates largely to getting in place a framework, or a set of frameworks, that supports rather than gets in the way of the changes that we seek. But frameworks, although necessary, are not the heart of the matter. What this conference has been concerned with is ways of identifying the expectations against which we can measure educational achievements, and ways in which educational achievements can be assessed. I believe that these questions are as important at the national level as at the level of the school or the LEAs.

They require us to look closely at the nature of the curriculum. For at the heart of *Better Schools* is the policy of raising standards of teaching and learning for pupils of all ages and abilities, including those who gain least from 11 years of schooling. The Government remains utterly committed to that goal. The place where that finally has to be achieved is, for the most part, the school itself, in the countless daily transactions between pupil and teacher. Is it any wonder that the assessment progress at this level is much more difficult? Let me remind you of some of the difficulties. It is easy to say, for example, that we wish to start by assessing standards in the most basic aspects of education, such as reading comprehension and arithmetic computation. But the work of the APU has shown that apparently slight changes in the phrasing of questions can produce widely differing results. Let us suppose, though, that the problem of *how* to assess progress is overcome; we still need to agree *what* to assess.

Here it is plain that there are many legitimate views about what it is that we should be trying to measure, and about the possible benefits and drawbacks of particular objectives in assessment. Yet even that does not exhaust the difficulties of the endeavour. The curriculum and methods of teaching are constantly evolving because the world in which the schools exist is ever-changing. Those changes bring with them, inescapably, changes also in forms of assessment.

The difficulty of describing accurately and unambiguously what we mean by standards of achievement across the curriculum at any one time, and in a way which seems likely to mean something in 5, 10 or 20 years' time, makes it extremely difficult even to begin to assess changes in standards. But we must nevertheless attempt to do so.

Conference papers have described, from different perspectives, the value of assessment. I need add only that it seems to me to be quite impossible to chart the future course of education in our schools unless we have a clear picture of where we are now, and how successful the efforts were that brought us to our present position. There is room for debate about what we should be assessing and how; there is no doubt in my mind — and it is important that the education service as a whole takes this to heart — that the enterprise itself is essential.

That has, I am glad to say, largely been taken as read in the papers that I have seen; they have concentrated on the technical issues arising, and on how schools and LEAs can and do keep a watch on the standards achieved as a means both of improving performance and of satisfying themselves that the appropriate standards are being achieved.

Part of the job of the holder of my office is to speak for the customers of the education system. I therefore note that parents, employers, taxpayers and ratepayers all have an important interest in the success of our schools. That interest extends beyond a general concern to see that the schools are doing a good job, into the area of how it is we can tell whether they are doing a good job.

It seems to me clear that we need a wide range of instruments, not only to enable LEAs and schools to choose the most appropriate forms for their particular circumstances, but also because assessment has many important aims and we cannot expect a single form of assessment to encompass them all equally well. Let me list some of those that strike me as particularly important — in no particular order and with no claim to originality:

— *first*, providing feedback to pupils, parents and teachers

— *second*, assessing pupils' progress

— *thirdly*, improvement in the motivation of pupils (and teachers)

— *fourthly*, the diagnosis of pupils' strengths and weaknesses

— *fifthly*, guidance about educational and vocational choices; and

— *sixthly*, the evaluation of the extent to which worthwhile curricular objectives are being achieved.

These aims are, or at least ought to be, envisaged by forms of assessment which have a national significance; for example public examinations. But I believe that the same aims should inform assessment at the local and at the school level.

I hope that this makes it plain why the Government has spent such a great deal of time over the past few years, in co-operation with its partners, on a range of initiatives on assessment at the national level: on trying to make the right changes to the public examinations at 16-plus, on promoting records of achievement, on supporting development work on graduated assessment and on the appraisal of teachers.

180

I know that many people feel that the role of examination results in assessing the performance of schools is overvalued. It is certainly true that examination results often receive great public attention; it is also true that they can be an important measure of standards. They will serve this purpose even more effectively when grade criteria are introduced. But it is also true that, for a number of reasons, examination results on their own are insufficient as a measure of the standards achieved and have little bearing on many aspects of school education, including the work of the primary schools. It is important that both these messages should be widely understood.

I hope that the publication of the conference papers will bring such issues to the attention of the education service and of a wider public. I am grateful for the ready response by so many people to my suggestion that this conference should take place, and particularly for the work of those who have prepared papers and who have attended and contributed to discussion.

I turn now to ways in which it seems to me that the holder of my office can and should contribute to the assessment process.

Curriculum

There are several important educational reasons for the Government's attempt to reach broad national agreement about the objectives of the curriculum, and the fact that such agreement might facilitate assessment of standards at the national level is by no means the primary purpose of the exercise. I believe that teachers will find it helpful to have clear statements of what is, and what is not, expected of them — statements that will, without imposing an inhibiting straitjacket on LEAs' or schools' exercise of their own statutory responsibilities for the curriculum, provide a supportive framework within which the individual school's curriculum can be developed and assessed. I believe also that the progression and continuity of pupils' programmes will be improved where objectives are clearly understood, and that parents and employers will find it valuable to be able to place the work of a particular school within the context of broadly agreed national objectives for the curriculum.

Nonetheless, it is, as I have suggested, impossible to assess progress, in any objective way, unless you have defined the goals towards which you are working. Indeed, I would go further and say that in principle meaningful assessment is possible only to the extent that there is a degree of agreement both about objectives and about the means of assessing progress towards them.

It is not for the Government, acting on its own, to lay down what such objectives should be. Yet the Government has — literally — a central part in the formulation of objectives. It is a partner in the education service, with certain national responsibilities in regard to education. It also has the job of trying to interpret the wishes of the customers of the service and of those who pay for it, as well as promoting what is professionally desirable. Against that background, it is the Government's task to promote the achievement of agreement about objectives, and to seek to set out the extent of the agreement reached as a guide to LEAs, schools, teachers, teacher trainers and examinations boards. It is also the Government's task to make clear the objectives which will be followed by the holder of my office in relation to the curriculum, and in the exercise of statutory functions such as those relating to the supply of teachers.

In the pursuit of these objectives the Government is in a position to promote specific developments. Examples of recent work on this basis include, of course, the Technical and Vocational Education Initiative (TVEI), the lower attaining pupils programme, the range of activities supported under education support grant (ESG) and under the in-service grants scheme, and support for the work of the Microelectronics Education Programme (MEP) and (with the local authority associations) of the School Curriculum Development Committee (SCDC).

The desirability of reaching national agreement on curricular objectives was one of the main themes of my speech to the North of England Education Conference at Sheffield in January 1984. Since then, I have had discussions with all the partners in the education service about how to work towards that end. The White Paper *Better Schools* set out the Government's views, and described the way in which we proposed to carry matters forward through the twin channels of Government policy statements and HMI's 'Curriculum Matters' papers, which would offer a professional elaboration of the issues raised by various areas and subjects within the curriculum. I want to make it clear that the Government takes a wide view of the curriculum, and therefore of assessment. Both are concerned not only with knowledge, skills and understanding, but also with values and attitudes, including behaviour and the preparation of pupils for adult life and employment.

The first of the policy statements, on *Science 5–16*[1], was published earlier this year and has been well received. We shall be following it up with others over the next two years or so: we hope that a paper on foreign languages will be available fairly soon. HMI have so far published five 'Curriculum Matters' papers, and have plans for a substantial number of others over the next couple of years. These papers, which are offered for comment — and have certainly provoked it — begin to define objectives for attainment by pupils at various ages, particularly 11 and 16.

---

[1] *DES: Science 5–16: a Statement of Policy.* HMSO, 1985.

Attainment in the primary phase

In this way the 'Curriculum Matters' papers are a contribution towards the aim, set out in *Better Schools*, of reaching 'a more precise definition... of what pupils of different abilities should understand, know and be able to do'. *Better Schools* acknowledged that this aim would not be an easy one to achieve. For one thing, attainment targets cannot be simply expressed if they are to apply to the whole ability range; for another, the type of definition and the degree of its precision will vary between elements of the curriculum. I believe that HMI have begun a very important process.

In taking the process further, I believe that we will find it instructive to examine a particular aspect of the curriculum in depth, to see what lessons can be learned about the value of different types of measurement of attainment. Such work would have the dual purpose of assisting the process of monitoring standards nationally and of helping LEAs and teachers in the discharge of their responsibilities. It seems most useful to concentrate initially on attainment in the primary phase, not only because much work is already in hand in the secondary phase (for example, in connection with the grade criteria for GCSE), but also because the very successes of schools in broadening the primary curriculum over the last 20 years mean that we have comparatively little information about what it is reasonable to expect pupils to achieve.

Let me make it quite clear that the purpose of this work would not in any sense be to devise 'national tests of attainment' at age 11. The evidence from HMI is that competence in, for example, language and mathematics is improved not by a narrow concentration on testable skills, but by offering a variety of contexts in which those skills can be applied. But I do believe that we need sensitive action which avoids this pitfall to be undertaken by LEAs and schools, making use of appropriate forms of assessment. It is this that I wish to promote.

I have no doubt that the sophisticated exercise that I have in mind will be difficult; I recognise that my goal may turn out not to be wholly achievable. But we should make the attempt: progress in this area will be of inestimable benefit to teachers and parents. Within the primary phase a significant amount of relevant work has been done in the field of mathematics, notably by the APU. I therefore propose that the Department should commission work, limited in the first instance to a feasibility study, on mathematics in the primary phase. The aim will be to bring together what is already known about pupils' present levels of attainment in mathematics, and to see how to build on that to develop assessment methods which schools and authorities could themselves use. We shall be keeping our partners in touch with the details of what we have in mind.

Appraising the performance of schools

In one sense, this work will be an extension of the Department's existing support for research and development in the field of assessment. Much evaluation and appraisal is properly the responsibility of teachers, schools and LEAs carrying out their proper functions. The role of the holder of my office, it seems to me, is to see that appropriate instruments and forms of assessment are available for use by the education service.

Is there a need for further research and the development of new techniques? We will all need time to digest what has been said at this conference before we can assess in detail where the priorities are. But I think that some areas for future work have begun to emerge.

I have already mentioned our proposal to make a start in developing some form of assessment of the achievements of primary school pupils. More widely, the Department is considering at the moment a number of proposals for research intended to throw further light on the in-school factors that affect the performance and achievement of pupils. We may need to consider also the extent to which the GCSE examinations, with the introduction of grade criteria, will permit judgements to be made about standards over time — the intractable problem which I mentioned earlier.

All that, with the ideas that have been discussed at this conference, sets a very full programme. I turn now to the services that the Government provides to assist with the evaluation and appraisal of the work of the schools.

The provision of evaluation and appraisal by the Government

The Government provides two distinct services to this end. The first is inspection through HMI. HMI inspect and assess quality and standards of both teaching and learning. This work is undertaken not just to inform the Government about the health of the education system as a whole; nor simply to provide those directly concerned with the institutions inspected with a basis for assessing and improving their current practice. HMI's work is also undertaken to inform the education system and the public at large about current standards, and to promote improvements throughout the system at all levels.

That is why HMI now publish and disseminate a range of documents, on broad and narrow topics, aimed at a wide readership. They are, I know, always looking for fresh ways of presenting their findings so as to enhance their important contribution to our understanding of the way the quality and achievements of the system change over time.

At the local level, I should perhaps note that although some HMI reports suggest changes in individual schools, HMI are nevertheless not the main agency involved in the process of identifying where there is need for improvement. LEAs and the schools themselves have the primary responsibility in this respect. I therefore welcome the attention given to whole school evaluation at earlier sessions of this conference. The recently issued joint statement on LEA advisory services made clear the large contribution that advisers make to this work. And at the level of the authority, it is the CEO who is responsible for the overall assessment of the institutions maintained; while at school level, heads and heads of department have the main part to play in the school's assessment of its own performance.

To return to central government's services, the Department also provides for the monitoring of pupil performance throughout the school system, in selected curriculum areas, through the work of the APU. Detailed reports on the Unit's findings are published. These are aimed, in the first instance, at informing those in LEAs and in teacher training institutions, who are in a position to promote change and improvement. The reports provide descriptions of pupils' performance, across the whole range of ability (outside special education), in a way which has not been attempted before. They show the tasks at which pupils succeed, and those which they find difficult; and they begin to explore the nature of the difficulties so that other agencies can seek ways of tackling them. A wide audience is also now being made aware of the results of the APU's surveys through reports designed for teachers. These attempt to set out the findings in a more readily digestible form. In addition, the Department has commissioned independent appraisals of the implications of the Unit's findings. The first of these, *New Perspectives on the Mathematics Curriculum*[1] was published in October this year.

Teaching standards

There is one area of provision in which the holder of my office has a direct responsibility for assessing quality: the training of teachers. This responsibility relates not only to the number of teachers to be trained, but also to the content of their training.

The quality and relevance of the initial training received by teachers entering the profession will have a vital bearing on the improvement of educational standards proposed in *Better Schools*. It is a responsibility of the holder of my office to approve courses of initial teacher training as being suitable for the professional preparation of teachers and the conferment of qualified teacher status. In order that courses may be assessed both consistently and rigorously, we have drawn up criteria for their approval and established the Council for the Accreditation of Teacher Education (CATE) to review all such courses against the

---

[1] Cambridge Institute of Education: *New Perspectives on the Mathematics Curriculum*. An independent appraisal of the outcomes of APU mathematics testing 1978–82. Assessment of Performance Unit, 1985.

criteria and make recommendations. In all cases the Council will take account of the findings of HMI visits to institutions and will have the benefit of the advice of HMI assessors.

CATE is now fully established. I am satisfied that it is taking a thorough, searching approach to its task. Moreover, it is clear that the criteria and the process of accreditation are already having a beneficial effect on the system as institutions adapt and develop courses. Both the Department and HMI will continue to monitor progress. But the improvement of initial teacher training cannot be a matter for central direction and assessment alone: schools, LEAs and the wider community also have a vital part to play, as is recognised in the criteria.

No course can be considered for approval unless it has the support of a widely representative local committee. Moreover, the criteria call for close working relationships between training institutions and schools. Tutors should maintain regular and frequent experience of classroom teaching. Practising schoolteachers should be involved in the development of courses, the selection of candidates, the training of students in institutions and the assessment of their teaching practice in schools. It is for LEAs to facilitate this interaction. Thus, while it is for the holder of my office to establish the necessary framework for the improvement of initial teacher training, for CATE to review courses and for HMI to monitor progress, it is for the schools, LEAs and the training institutions themselves to implement change and secure the improvements on which so much else depends.

Teaching quality is therefore as much a matter for local as for national policy. Initial training cannot equip a teacher for a life-time's teaching as the curriculum evolves, or for the variety of responsibilities which a teacher undertakes as his or her career develops. Hence the importance of in-service training as an instrument for improving the quality of teaching. *Better Schools* makes clear that the Government's policies for improving standards in schools will make increased demands in particular on teachers' practical teaching skills, their breadth and depth of subject knowledge and their knowledge of and skills in assessment. Extensive in-service training will be needed to equip teachers to respond to these demands.

Significant resources are already invested in in-service training. It is widely agreed that not all are used to best advantage. The Government's plans for a new specific grant to support local authority expenditure on most aspects of in-service training are designed primarily to help secure more purposeful and systematic planning of in-service training. More effective in-service training requires more systematic approaches to identifying the in-service training needs of individual teachers, and to matching those needs with appropriate provision in a way which is cost effective and compatible with an assessment of priorities for such training by schools and the LEA.

Although HMI will monitor progress, the main burden of the difficult task of assessing the value added by in-service training, and whether the most is being made of available resources, will properly fall to the LEA in close co-operation with its schools and teachers. The holder of my office has a role to play in identifying key national priorities for in-service training: however the main thrust of the Government's policy in this area is to support and promote existing good practice in LEAs.

Closely associated with in-service training, and with the career development of teachers, is the need for LEAs regularly to appraise the performance of their teachers. A sensitively worked out scheme, carefully introduced and embodying adequate safeguards for the individual, would, I am confident, help all teachers realise their full professional potential by providing them with better job satisfaction, more appropriate in-service training and better planned career development.

I repeat that I envisage 'a sensitively worked out scheme, carefully introduced, and embodying safeguards for the individual'. I understand the concern that has been expressed to me about the possibility that annual appraisal procedures might be directly linked to merit pay or annual increments, or be used in other ways by headteachers to give instant rewards or penalties. That is quite definitely not the sort of arrangement I have in mind — nor do I know of any local authority that would wish to use an appraisal scheme in such a way.

But I do believe that the findings from appraisal interviews would lead to better informed promotion decisions by schools and LEAs. This must be an advance on what some of the unions have described as the 'lottery' of the current promotion arrangements, informed as they are by haphazard, informal unsystematic appraisal of performance. Moreover, I would expect any appraisal scheme to extend to the appraisal of headteachers.

I am often told, too, that a successful appraisal scheme will depend on teachers being properly prepared and trained, and having sufficient time to allocate to the appraisal process. I accept that. The time requirement is one of the considerations to be taken into account in studying the numbers of teachers needed in the longer-term. The training requirement could become a priority within the new arrangements envisaged for in-service training. But before we can plan satisfactorily for these developments we need the pilot projects the Department has been seeking to set up.

As you will know, and as foreshadowed in *Better Schools*, the Government plans during this session of Parliament [1985–86] to enable the holder of my office, in appropriate circumstances, to require such appraisal to be carried out. I understand the concern that has been expressed about this, too, along with the view that appraisal systems need to be introduced in co-operation with those who are to be appraised. I agree with that. I therefore stress that what is intended is an enabling power. Whether it will be used will depend upon circumstances. I very much hope that regular teacher-appraisal will be introduced voluntarily — as it can be now by agreement between employer and employee. Considerable effort has been made over a long period in pursuit of an agreement incorporating the introduction of systematic arrangements for appraisal. This effort has sadly not yet borne fruit. Just as sad, I think, is the unwillingness, until now, of the teacher unions to join in with the local authorities and the Department in the preparatory fieldwork which I am sure is necessary if we are to work out a mutually acceptable form of appraisal for teachers. The money set aside by the Government for an ESG in this area remains untouched. But I have not given up hope of practical co-operation in this area, because I am more convinced than ever that appraisal would be a good thing both for standards in the education service and also for the professional development of teachers.

Why does the holder of my office need the proposed power? One reason is that progress in this area has been painfully slow. It may be appropriate to use the new power in association with new arrangements for in-service training to promote more rapid progress. But quite apart from that consideration, it may well be desirable to have a national framework within which local appraisal schemes would operate — after all, the current arrangements for the probation of new teachers are national and this has long been accepted as a means of providing for consistency and fairness. We have no national blueprint to impose. The Government position is that teacher-appraisal should largely be conducted at the level of the individual school by the teachers themselves. It would be done in accordance with general arrangements introduced and monitored by LEAs in accordance with national guidelines worked out in consultation between teachers, employers and the Department. I hope that this conference will mark a new beginning for this co-operative venture.

Conclusion

My intention has been to describe the ways in which the Government can lead debate about assessment, make information available to inform that debate and improve the practice of assessment at the national, local and school level. But, to a very large extent, the place where assessment and appraisal matters most is in the LEA and in the school. An enormous amount must inevitably depend on the work of the many thousands of teachers, advisers and others engaged in this work. It is their work that this conference has mainly been about. I hope that, through the publication of the papers discussed, the conference will prove to be useful not only to those who have been present, but also to a much wider audience. Assessment, evaluation, appraisal and monitoring are not the only activities which improve standards. But they are essential. That is why at every level we need all to work at making them activities which are not only difficult and challenging, but fruitful.

BIBLIOGRAPHY

Certain of the publications mentioned in the conference papers were on display during the event, together with the documents listed below, which are further sources of relevant information.

The list includes both priced and unpriced publications. A *DES Free publications list/order form* is available from Publications Despatch Centre, DES, Honeypot Lane, Canons Park, Stanmore, Middlesex HA7 1AZ; an HMI list is also obtainable from this source. Addresses for enquiries concerning publications issued on behalf of the DES by HMSO are given on the back cover.

NOTE: Some of the titles listed were published by the DES jointly with other UK Education Departments.

Advanced Supplementary (AS) levels: a summary specification. DES, 1985

Annual Report 1984–85, SCDC (School Curriculum Development Committee), 1985*

Annual Report 1984–85, SEC (Secondary Examinations Council), 1985*

APU (Assessment of Performance Unit) *Newsletter.* No 7 Spring 1985. DES. (Further details of APU publications are available from APU, Room 4/77A, Elizabeth House, York Road, London SE1 7PH.)

APU What it is, How it Works. Publicity leaflet. DES, 1984

Better Schools. A summary [*of the White Paper, Cmnd 9469, HMSO*]. DES, 1985

Blueprint for Numeracy. An employers' guide to Cockcroft. DES, 1983

CPVE (Certificate of Pre-Vocational Education) *Gives You a Step Up.* Leaflet and poster. DES, 1985. (Other titles in preparation.)

Education Observed. A review of the first six months of published reports by HM Inspectors. DES, 1984

Education Observed 2. A review of published reports by HM Inspectors on primary schools and 11–16 and 12–16 comprehensive schools. DES, 1984

English from 5 *to* 16. HMI 'Curriculum Matters' series No 1. HMSO, 1984

Foreign Language Performance in Schools. APU Report on 1983 survey of French, German and Spanish. DES, 1985

GCSE (General Certificate of Secondary Education): *The National Criteria.* HMSO, 1985

GCSE: *A General Introduction.* HMSO, 1985

GCSE: *The New Exam System at* 16-*plus.* Leaflet and poster. DES, 1985

GCSE: SEC poster. SEC, 1985

---

* Available from: Information Section, Newcombe House, 45 Notting Hill Gate, London W11 3JB.

BIBLIOGRAPHY

GCSE: *The Development of Grade Criteria for the GCSE*. An explanatory leaflet. SEC, 1985

GCSE: *Differentiated Assessment in GCSE*. Working papers, SEC, 1985

Hancock, Sir David (Permanent Secretary, DES): 'Staff Appraisal in Schools and Colleges — A view from DES'. Talk to the Education for Industrial Society, 25 February 1985. DES, Press Notice 34/85

HM Inspectors Today: Standards in Education. DES, 1983

Home Background Variables in Education. Report of a research project commissioned by the DES and conducted at the University of Leeds. University of Leeds, 1984. *Summary report*. DES, 1985. (Available from Room 4/91, Elizabeth House, York Road, London SE1 7PH.)

Home Economics from 5 to 16. HMI 'Curriculum Matters' series No 5. HMSO, 1985

How Well Can 15-year-olds Write? DES report on APU findings. DES, 1983

Language Performance in Schools. APU 1982 Primary Survey Report. DES, 1984

Link. SCDC newsletter (published termly).

Mathematics from 5 to 16. HMI 'Curriculum Matters' series No 3. HMSO, 1985

Mathematical Development. A review of (APU) monitoring in mathematics — 1978 to 1982 (two parts). Report from the NFER to the DES *et al*, 1985

Modular Approaches to the Secondary Curriculum. Curriculum Issues No 1. SCDC, 1985

Monitoring Foreign Languages. APU publicity leaflet. DES, 1984

Monitoring Language. APU publicity leaflet. DES, 1984

Monitoring Mathematics. APU publicity leaflet. DES, 1984

Monitoring Science. APU publicity leaflet, DES, 1984

Music from 5 *to* 16. HMI 'Curriculum Matters' series No 4. HMSO, 1985

Practical Testing at Ages 11, 13 *and* 15. APU Science Report for Teachers No 6. DES, 1985*

Project Profiles (eleven projects). SCDC, 1984/85

SCDC: an Introduction. Explanatory leaflet. SCDC, 1984

SEC News. (published termly).

Science at Age 11. APU Science Report for Teachers No 1. DES, 1984*

Science At Age 13. APU Science Report for Teachers No 3. DES, 1984*

Science At Age 15. APU Science Report for Teachers No 5. DES, 1985*

Standards in English Schools. NCES (National Council for Educational Standards) Research Report No 1. NCES, 1983. (Available from 1 Hinchley Way, Esher, Surrey, KT10 0BD.)

Standards in English Schools. NCES Research Report No 2. NCES, 1985

---

* Available from the Association for Science Education, College Lane, Hatfield, Hertfordshire AL10 9AA.

Standards of Performance — Expectations and Reality. APU Occasional Paper No 3. DES, 1984

Wilkinson, D A: 'How the DES Views the Future of Appraisal in Schools and Colleges: An update from the Department'. Talk to the Industrial Society, 3 July 1985. DES, Press Notice, 171/85

CONFERENCE DELEGATES

Local Education Authorities in England and Wales

Other organisations and institutions represented*

Assistant Masters and Mistresses Association
Association of County Councils
Association of Metropolitan Authorities
Campaign for the Advancement of State Education
Catholic Education Council
Church of England Board of Education
Confederation of British Industry
Council of Local Education Authorities
Danbury Park Management Centre
Department of Education for Northern Ireland
Engineering Employers' Federation
Further Education Staff College, Coombe Lodge
Head Masters' Conference
Hirst High School, Ashington
Independent Schools Joint Council
J Sainsbury plc
Local Authorities' Conditions of Service Advisory Board
Morley Victoria Junior and Infants School, Leeds
National Association of Governors and Managers
National Association of Head Teachers
National Association of Schoolmasters/Union of Women Teachers
National Confederation of Parent-Teacher Associations
National Council for Special Education
National Development Centre for School Management Training
National Foundation for Educational Research
National Union of Teachers
Professional Association of Teachers
Putteridge High School and Community College, Luton
Remploy Ltd
Roehampton Institute of Higher Education
School Curriculum Development Committee
Scottish Education Department
Secondary Heads Association
The Industrial Society
The Open University
Thurston Upper School, Suffolk
Understanding Industry
Watergall Junior School, Peterborough
Welsh Joint Education Committee
Welsh Office Education Department

* *in addition to the DES and HMI.*

Printed in the UK for HMSO by Hobbs the Printers of Southampton
(50) Dd738227 C35 3/86 G380